Washington Legal Research

Second Edition

CAROLINA ACADEMIC PRESS
LEGAL RESEARCH SERIES

Suzanne E. Rowe, Series Editor

᪐

Arizona—Tamara S. Herrera

Arkansas—Coleen M. Barger

California—Hether C. Macfarlane & Suzanne E. Rowe

Connecticut—Jessica G. Hynes

Florida, Third Edition—Barbara J. Busharis & Suzanne E. Rowe

Georgia—Nancy P. Johnson, Elizabeth G. Adelman & Nancy J. Adams

Idaho—Tenielle Fordyce-Ruff & Suzanne E. Rowe

Illinois—Mark E. Wojcik

Kansas—Joseph A. Custer & Christopher L. Steadham

Louisiana—Mary Garvey Algero

Michigan—Pamela Lysaght

Missouri—Wanda M. Temm & Julie M. Cheslik

New York—Elizabeth G. Adelman & Suzanne E. Rowe

Ohio—Katherine L. Hall & Sara Sampson

Oregon, Second Edition—Suzanne E. Rowe

Pennsylvania—Barbara J. Busharis & Bonny L. Tavares

Tennessee—Sibyl Marshall & Carol McCrehan Parker

Texas—Spencer L. Simons

Washington, Second Edition—Julie Heintz-Cho, Tom Cobb
& Mary A. Hotchkiss

᪐

Washington Legal Research

Second Edition

Julie Heintz-Cho
Tom Cobb
Mary A. Hotchkiss

Suzanne E. Rowe, Series Editor

CAROLINA ACADEMIC PRESS
Durham, North Carolina

Library of Congress Cataloging-in-Publication Data

Heintz-Cho, Julie.
Washington legal research / Julie Heintz-Cho, Tom Cobb, Mary
A. Hotchkiss. -- 2nd ed.
    p. cm.
Includes bibliographical references and index.
ISBN 978-1-59460-718-9 (alk. paper)
1. Legal research--Washington (State) I. Cobb, Tom. II.
Hotchkiss, Mary A. III. Title.
KFW75.H45 2009
340.072'0797--dc22

                                                    2009012170

            CAROLINA ACADEMIC PRESS
                700 Kent Street
         Durham, North Carolina 27701
          Telephone (919) 489-7486
              Fax (919) 493-5668
              www.cap-press.com

        Printed in the United States of America
                  2021 Printing

Summary of Contents

Contents

Contents

List of Tables and Figures

Tables

Figures

Series Note

The Legal Research Series published by Carolina Academic Press includes an increasing number of titles from states around the country. The goal of each book is to provide law students, practitioners, paralegals, college students, laypeople, and librarians with the essential elements of legal research in each state. Unlike more bibliographic texts, the Legal Research Series books seek to explain concisely both the sources of state law research and the process for conducting legal research effectively.

Preface to the First Edition

This book is part of a series of research books published by Carolina Academic Press. Each book in the series explains how to conduct legal research in a particular state. Although this book is specific to Washington, some of the material draws from earlier books in the series. This is most evident in the ordering of the chapters and in the explanations of federal materials. I am sure I speak for all of the series' authors when I say "thank you" to Professor Suzanne Rowe for her contribution. Professor Rowe is the author of one of the first books in the series, *Oregon Legal Research*, and a co-author of *Florida Legal Research*. She deserves much credit for developing this content and for providing a template for other authors to follow.

As with all of the books in Carolina's series, the primary audience for *Washington Legal Research* is first-year law students. However, the information in the book would be no less valuable for paralegal students, new associates, and even more experienced practitioners new to Washington.

One major difference between this book and earlier books in the series is that this book incorporates online research into each chapter. Although members of the legal research and writing community disagree about when and how to teach electronic research, computer research is becoming the norm in both law schools and law firms. In our program at Seattle University School of Law, we incorporate online research into our teaching as soon as possible, and the book follows this format.

In writing the book, I tried to make the explanations understandable for those new to legal research. Too many times, research books and legal research teachers "forget" that most students are starting from a point of virtually no knowledge of legal resources and the legal research process. Experienced attorneys and students familiar with research fundamentals may find some of the book's information very basic; nevertheless, I erred on the side of reinforcing what some may already know rather than alienating those who are just beginning their venture into legal research. For those who would just like to read selected chapters, Appendix C provides a quick reference to some commonly used Washington legal research abbreviations that may not be explained in the chapters you select to read. In addition, for researchers who may want more detailed information than this book provides, Appendix B contains a list of recommended texts.

Julie A. Heintz
January 2005

Preface to the Second Edition

We thank Suzanne Rowe for developing this useful series of legal research books and for giving us the opportunity to participate. We would also like to thank Julie Heintz-Cho for writing an exceptionally readable first edition, which we have used successfully in our classes.

Washington Legal Research was first published in 2005 and was innovative in its focus on online research. Since then, however, aspects of the book have become dated due in part to the rapid increase in the availability of legal research materials online and in part to changes in how commercial websites deliver content. We have tried to bring the book up to date and to generalize some of the descriptions so that it can remain up to date for as long as possible.

In addition to updating the book, we took the opportunity to re-order some of the chapters so that they matched more closely the steps most law teachers now recommend to budding legal researchers. Accordingly, the book now begins by explaining how to research secondary sources, then statutes, then case law and other materials.

Finally, we have sought to continue the tradition of concision and ease of use, hallmarks of this legal research series and the first edition of this book.

Tom Cobb
Mary A. Hotchkiss
December 2008

Acknowledgments

We are grateful to Professor Suzanne Rowe and our colleagues at both Seattle University School of Law and the University of Washington School of Law. We also thank the reference librarians at both law schools for their assistance with this book. We thank Kelly Fahl, Paul Tassin, and Jason Voss for providing valuable research support. Finally, we thank Kevin Francis, Sarah Kaltsounis, and Mary Whisner for their helpful comments on drafts and their professional and personal encouragement.

JAH-C
TC
MAH

Washington Legal Research

Second Edition

Chapter 1

Research Fundamentals

I. Introduction

One of the key ways a lawyer can assist clients is to conduct effective research. The Washington Rules of Professional Conduct, which cover all aspects of legal practice in Washington, provide that "[a] lawyer shall provide competent representation to a client. Competent representation requires the legal knowledge, skill, thoroughness and preparation reasonably necessary for the representation."[1] A large part of this knowledge and preparation comes from legal research.

The fundamentals of legal research are the same in every American jurisdiction, though the details vary. While some variations are minor, others require specialized knowledge of the resources available and how those resources are organized and accessed. This book focuses on the resources available in Washington and processes for using them. It also contains brief explanations of federal research and research into other states' law.

Legal analysis is difficult. This realization may come when you first walk into a law library or when you log onto a legal website and become overwhelmed by the number of sources and by the thought of doing legal research. Yet, the basic process of legal research is not complicated, and it can help improve your legal analysis skills.

For most sources, whether in print or online, you will begin your research with a table of contents or an index, find entries that appear relevant, read those sections of the text, and then find out whether

---

1. RPC 1.1.

more recent information is available. Or you will search particular databases using words likely to appear in the text of relevant documents. Legal analysis is interwoven throughout this process. Which words will you look up in the table of contents or the index? How will you decide whether an index entry looks promising? How will you choose relevant words and construct a search most likely to produce the documents you need? When you read a document, how will you determine whether it is relevant to your client's situation? How will you learn whether more recent material changed the law or merely applied it to a new situation? The answer to each of these questions requires legal analysis.

As you do more legal research, you will notice improvement in your legal analysis skills; similarly, as you learn more about legal analysis, you will notice improvement in your legal research skills. This book's focus is legal research, but to advance this cyclical learning process, it also addresses some fundamental concepts of legal analysis.

This book does not provide a blueprint of every resource available; many resources contain their own detailed explanation in a preface or a "help" section. Instead, this book is more like a "quick set-up" guide or manual, introducing the resources needed at each step of the research process and explaining how to use them.

II. Types and Sources of Legal Authority

Before researching the law, you must be clear about the goal of your search. To begin, you will want to find the constitutional provisions, statutes, administrative rules, and judicial opinions that control, or potentially control, your client's situation. In other words, you are searching for primary, mandatory authority.

A. Key Concepts

Legal professionals generally divide legal authority along two lines. The first distinguishes primary authority from secondary authority.

Primary authority refers to law produced by government bodies with law-making power. Legislatures write statutes; courts write judicial opinions; and administrative agencies write rules or regulations. *Secondary authority* includes all other sources, such as legal encyclopedias, practice guides, and law review articles. These secondary sources are designed to help you understand the law and locate primary authority.

The second division distinguishes mandatory from persuasive authority. *Mandatory authority* is binding on the court that would decide a conflict if the situation were litigated. In a question of Washington law, mandatory authority (also called *binding authority*) includes Washington's constitution, statutes enacted by the Washington legislature, opinions of the Washington Supreme Court and the Washington Court of Appeals, and Washington administrative regulations. *Persuasive authority*, on the other hand, is not binding, but may be followed if relevant and well reasoned. Authority may be considered persuasive if it is from a different jurisdiction or from a lower court, or if it is not produced by a law-making body. In a question of Washington law, examples of persuasive authority would include a similar California statute, an opinion of an Oregon or Alaska state court, and a law review article.

Within the category of primary, mandatory authority, there is an interlocking hierarchy of law. The constitution of each state is the supreme law of that state, and it trumps other laws. If a statute is on point, that statute comes next in the hierarchy, followed by administrative rules. Judicial opinions may interpret statutes or rules but may not disregard them. A judicial opinion may, however, decide that a statute violates the constitution or that a rule oversteps its bounds. If there is no constitutional provision, statute, or administrative rule on point, the issue may be controlled by *common law* or judge-made law.

B. Court Systems

Legal research often requires reading judicial opinions, and so researchers need to understand the court system. The basic structure includes a trial court, an intermediate court of appeals, and an ultimate appellate court, often called the "supreme" court.[2] These courts exist at both the state and federal levels.

1. Washington Courts

a. Trial Courts

In Washington, there are three types of trial courts: municipal courts, district courts, and superior courts. Municipal and district courts are called courts of *limited jurisdiction* because they have the power to hear only certain types of cases, usually those that involve less serious offenses or relatively small amounts of money. For example, a municipal court's jurisdiction is generally limited to criminal and traffic offenses arising from violations of local ordinances; the jurisdiction of district courts is limited to civil cases up to $75,000, small claims cases, criminal and gross misdemeanors, and traffic citations. Municipal courts are created by cities or towns, while district courts are county courts.

Superior courts are called courts of *general jurisdiction* because they can hear any type of civil or criminal case. These courts also hear appeals from the courts of limited jurisdiction. Superior courts are grouped into single or multi-county districts. For example, King County has its own district; Island County and San Juan County are grouped together in one district.

b. The Court of Appeals

Washington's intermediate court of appeals is called the Washington Court of Appeals.[3] The Court of Appeals has three divisions: Division I is located in Seattle, Division II is located in Tacoma, and Division III is located in Spokane. Each of these divisions is made up of

---

2. For brevity, the following description omits tribal courts. Information on tribal law is available on the State's website at http://access.wa.gov, under the "Government" link, and in Chapter 9 of *Washington Legal Researcher's Deskbook 3d* (see Appendix B for more information on this resource).

3. Before 1969, Washington's judicial system consisted of two tiers: trial courts and the Washington Supreme Court. The Court of Appeals was created in 1969, adding a third tier.

Table 1.1 Washington Court of Appeals

Division I (Seattle)	Number of Judges	Counties Included
Electoral district 1	6 judges	King County
Electoral district 2	2 judges	Snohomish County
Electoral district 3	2 judges	Island, San Juan, Skagit, and Whatcom Counties
Division II (Tacoma)	**Number of Judges**	**Counties Included**
Electoral district 1	3 judges	Pierce County
Electoral district 2	2 judges	Clallam, Grays Harbor, Jefferson, Kitsap, Mason, and Thurston Counties
Electoral district 3	2 judges	Clark, Cowlitz, Lewis, Pacific, Skamania, and Wahkiakum Counties
Division III (Spokane)	**Number of Judges**	**Counties Included**
Electoral district 1	2 judges	Ferry, Lincoln, Okanogan, Pend Oreille, Spokane, and Stevens Counties
Electoral district 2	1 judge	Adams, Asotin, Benton, Columbia, Franklin, Garfield, Grant, Walla Walla, and Whitman Counties
Electoral district 3	2 judges	Chelan, Douglas, Kittias, Klickitat, and Yakima Counties

Source: The Administrative Office of The Courts (Washington), www.courts.wa.gov.

three electoral districts. Table 1.1 shows the number of judges elected from each district and the counties located within each district.

Each Court of Appeals division hears appeals from all of the superior courts located in the division. For example, Division I hears cases appealed from the superior courts in King County, Snohomish County, Island County, San Juan County, Skagit County,

and Whatcom County. Unlike at a trial court, where only one judge
hears a case, at the Court of Appeals, a three-judge panel hears
each case. Although Court of Appeals judges rarely hear cases from
outside their division, they hear appeals from all courts within their
division.

c. The Supreme Court

The Supreme Court of Washington sits in Olympia and has nine
justices.[4] There are no divisions or districts of the Supreme Court,
and the Supreme Court sits *en banc* (all of the justices hear each case).
Unlike the Court of Appeals, which must hear every appeal filed, the
Supreme Court has discretion to decide which cases it hears, and parties must *petition for review* to ask the Supreme Court to hear their
case. The Supreme Court will accept such a petition only if (1) the
Court of Appeals decision conflicts with a Supreme Court decision,
(2) the Court of Appeals decision conflicts with a decision of another
Court of Appeals division, (3) the petition involves a significant state
or federal constitutional question, or (4) the petition involves an issue
of "substantial public interest" that should be decided by the Supreme
Court.[5]

The website for the Washington judiciary is www.courts.wa.gov. It
contains a wealth of information, including links to the appellate and
trial courts; an explanation of state courts; links to court personnel
and court forms; and recent opinions.

2. Other State Courts

Not all states have a three-tier court system like Washington's.
Some states have no intermediate appellate court. Also, in some court
systems the "supreme" court is not the highest court. In New York,
for example, the trial courts are called supreme courts and the highest court is called the Court of Appeals. Because of differences like

---

4. In general, a judge on the highest court is called a "justice" while a
judge on a lower court is called a "judge."
5. *See* Wash. Rule of Appellate Practice 13.4.

these, if you are working on a legal problem in another state, make sure you learn about that state's court system. Government websites and citation manuals, such as *The Bluebook* or the *ALWD Citation Manual* provide good starting points to learn about other states' judiciaries.

3. Federal Courts

In the federal judicial system, the trial courts are called United States District Courts. There are ninety-four district courts in the federal system, with each district drawn from a particular state. States like Washington, with large populations and relatively high caseloads, are subdivided into smaller geographic regions. Washington has two federal districts: the Eastern District of Washington and the Western District of Washington. States with smaller populations have only one district. For example, the entire state of Oregon is one federal district.

Intermediate appellate courts in the federal system are called United States Courts of Appeals. Each federal circuit has a federal court of appeals. Twelve of these circuits are based on geographic jurisdiction. These twelve consist of eleven numbered circuits covering all the states and a twelfth covering the District of Columbia. The thirteenth federal circuit, called the Federal Circuit, hears appeals from district courts in all the other circuits on issues related to patent law and from certain specialized courts and agencies. A map showing the federal circuits is available on the federal judiciary website at www.uscourts.gov (under the "Court Links" tab). You can also find circuit maps in the front of the *Federal Supplement* and the *Federal Reporter*, books in which cases decided by federal courts are published.

Washington is in the Ninth Circuit. This means that appeals from Washington federal district courts are heard by the United States Court of Appeals for the Ninth Circuit. This circuit encompasses Alaska, Arizona, California, Hawaii, Idaho, Montana, Nevada, Oregon, and Washington, as well as Guam and the Northern Mariana Islands.

The highest court in the federal system is the United States Supreme Court. It decides cases concerning the United States Constitution and federal statutes. The United States Supreme Court has the last word on the meaning of the federal constitution and other federal questions but does not have the final say on matters of purely state law; that authority rests with the highest court of each state. Like the Washington Supreme Court, the United States Supreme Court has discretion to decide which cases it hears. Parties who wish to appear in the United States Supreme Court must file a *petition for certiorari* asking for review, and the Court decides whether to grant certiorari based on criteria similar to those used by the Washington Supreme Court.[6]

The website for the federal judiciary contains court addresses, explanations of jurisdiction, and other helpful information. The address is www.uscourts.gov.

III. Overview of the Research Process

Conducting effective legal research requires developing and following a process. The goal of the research process is to find the legal authority necessary to analyze a legal problem completely and competently. The outline in Table 1.2 presents one effective approach to the research process.

You should customize this basic process for each research project and learn to use research tools flexibly. Depending on your project, you may not need to follow each step, or you may need to vary the order of the steps. For example, if you already know that a controlling statute exists, you should begin your research by looking at that statute (and sources that refer to it). Similarly, you may not need to perform a terms and connectors search because secondary materials and statutory annotations will lead you to the primary law you need, which you should then update.

---

6. *See* Sup. Ct. R. 10 (2007).

Table 1.2 Overview of the Research Process

1. Generate a list of *research terms*.

2. Do background reading in *secondary sources*, including encyclopedias, practice aids, and law review articles.

3. Find controlling *statutes, rules*, or *constitutional provisions* by searching in an annotated code. Use the *references to judicial decisions* that follow a statute or constitutional provision to find controlling cases.

4. Use a *digest* or an *online digest equivalent* to find citations to cases. If necessary, run a search in an online database. Refine analysis as needed.

5. *Update* your legal authorities to ensure that they have not been repealed, reversed, modified, or otherwise changed (this is also called "Shepardizing" or "KeyCiting").

6. *Assess* your research results. If the question is answered or the deadline is imminent, outline your legal analysis and begin writing your document.

A. Legal Sources: Key Concepts

Researchers must become familiar with some of the general characteristics of legal sources to feel comfortable using them. The following sections describe some of these characteristics.

1. Citation

A *citation* is a reference to an authority. In legal writing, citations serve several purposes, including showing the reader the weight of the authority (e.g., mandatory or persuasive) and telling the reader where to find the information. To *cite* means to refer to an authority. In law review articles, citations appear in footnotes; in legal memos and briefs, citations generally appear in the text, after each sentence requiring support. Table 1.3 shows two citations as they would ap-

Table 1.3 Citation Examples

Citation to a statute:	RCW 9A.52.020
Citation to a case:	*State v. Chiariello,* 66 Wn. App. 241, 831 P.2d 1119 (1992)

pear in a document filed with a Washington court, in the format prescribed by the Washington State Reporter of Decisions.[7]

In the first citation above, "RCW" is an abbreviation for *Revised Code of Washington.* The numbers following that abbreviation refer to the title (9A), chapter (52), and section (020) where the statute can be found in the official code. "State v. Chiariello" describes the parties in the case and is the case's title. The abbreviation "Wn. App." represents the *official reporter* where cases from the Washington Court of Appeals are published. The numbers surrounding the abbreviation refer to the volume of the official reporter and the page on which the case begins. The second set of numbers, also called a *parallel citation,* refers to a different set of volumes, a regional reporter, containing the case. Parallel citations are often provided in legal writing so that courts or law offices will be able to find cases no matter which set of reporters they have access to. The practice has become somewhat anachronistic now that most courts and law offices have online access to cases, but it is still followed in many jurisdictions, including Washington.

---

7. Most citations used in this book follow the rules from the *Style Sheet* used by the Washington courts. The abbreviations under these rules are sometimes different from the rules in *The Bluebook,* the *ALWD Manual,* and the rules from other state courts. For example, the *Revised Code of Washington* is abbreviated "Wash. Rev. Code" under *The Bluebook* and the *ALWD Manual* and "RCW" under the *Style Sheet.* A court rule requires all papers filed with the court to follow the *Style Sheet.* The current *Style Sheet* (February 19, 2009) is available at www.courts.wa.gov/appellate_trial_courts/supreme/?fa=atc_supreme.style.

2. Volume

A *volume* simply means a book. Legal sources often come in *multivolume sets*, meaning that there is more than one book in the set. In multivolume sets, the publisher will usually assign each volume its own *volume number*. Publishers update print resources using *pocket parts*, pamphlets issued once or twice a year and inserted at the back of each volume, or issue a free-standing paperback supplement when a pamphlet is too large to insert in a volume.

3. Table of Contents

A *table of contents* in a legal source is similar to a table of contents in any other type of source — it lists chapters and sections in a source and the pages on which those chapters and sections start. However, tables of contents in legal sources tend to be far more detailed and, therefore, more useful as research tools than those in non-legal sources. A table of contents is generally less detailed than an index, and the entries appear in an outline format (rather than in alphabetical order). Many online sources now include tables of contents with hyperlinks to chapters or articles. If you are using sources online, be sure to check whether they include tables of contents.

4. Index

An *index* in a legal source is the same as an index in any other type of resource. It is an alphabetical list of topics, words, or other items found in a source, and the place (often the page number) where the source discusses that topic. In legal sources, indexes usually take up several pages, and can often span several volumes. The level of detail and extensive cross-referencing in legal indexes make them especially powerful research tools.

Indexes often appear at the end of the volume or, in sources consisting of more than one volume, in separate volumes at the end of the set. Online indexes are particularly useful because they are searchable, but not all online sources have them. Searching in an online index is often far more efficient, reliable, and cost-effective than searching the full text of the document. Indeed, if the electronic version of your source lacks an index, consider using a print version so that you can take advantage of index searching.

5. Database

A *database* is a structured collection of information, usually in the form of individual documents or records. The terminology used by online providers will vary. Terms include database, source, library, and file.

On Westlaw, databases are each assigned an abbreviated title known as a *database identifier*. For example, WA-CS contains Washington state case law. If you know the database identifier for the collection of sources you want, you can type the identifier in the "Search for a Database" box to begin your search. In this book, Westlaw database identifiers will be included in parentheses following selected resources. On LexisNexis, databases are issued an abbreviated title known as a "File-Name" or "Source." The LexisNexis default, however, prompts users to access the source through cascading directory menus. The current path to Washington cases on LexisNexis is "Washington > Find Cases > WA State Cases, Combined."

B. Organization of This Text

The remainder of this book explains how to conduct legal research in a variety of sources. Most chapters in the book begin by explaining how to conduct research in print and then how to do the same kind of research using online sources. For that reason, Chapter 2 provides a brief introduction to essential research tools and techniques.

Because the research process often begins with secondary sources, Chapter 3 provides an overview of key secondary sources. The chapters that follow discuss researching various kinds of primary authority. Chapter 4 describes the process for researching statutes and the Washington Constitution; Chapter 5 describes judicial opinions and reporters. Chapter 6 explains how to use case finding tools such as digests and citators to find judicial opinions and other sources. Chapter 7 explains how to update legal authority using citators. Chapter 8 addresses administrative law, and Chapter 9 explains how to do legislative history research.

Chapter 10 builds on previous chapters and discusses research strategies and how to organize research results. You may prefer to skim that chapter now and refer to it frequently, even though a number of references in it may not become clear until you have read the intervening chapters.

Appendix A provides an overview of the conventions lawyers follow when citing legal authority in their documents. Appendix B contains a selected bibliography of legal research texts. Appendix C contains a list of commonly used Washington legal abbreviations.

As you read, keep in mind that this book only provides an introduction to Washington legal research. Even after reading this book, you will no doubt have questions about research techniques and sources. One of the best ways to continue learning about legal research is to ask for assistance from a reference librarian. Reference librarians can save you hours of research time: they can help you get started, find additional sources, and confirm that you are finding the best sources. Asking questions is the sign of an efficient researcher.

Chapter 2

Legal Research Tools and Techniques

I. Introduction

Law is a highly structured field of information with multiple systems and sophisticated research tools. For years, to use these systems and tools, researchers had to go to the library and either find books or use dedicated workstations to access online legal materials. But now legal information is increasingly digital, and researchers have access to extensive databases available 24 hours a day from virtually anywhere in the world.

The volume and availability of information can be overwhelming and carries with it certain hazards. Researchers accustomed to search engines like Google may initially feel comfortable searching LexisNexis and Westlaw, but they soon realize that navigating these immense collections of databases requires more sophisticated searching methods than they were accustomed to. Indeed, the sheer volume of legal materials available can feed researchers' insecurities and prompt them to question whether they have checked all the appropriate sources and found everything they need. To deal with these hazards and insecurities, every beginning legal researcher needs a strategy. That strategy is introduced here and explained further in Chapter 10.

II. Today's Research Environment

Thirty years ago, legal research revolved around print resources, and publishers developed sophisticated research tools to help attorneys identify and understand cases, statutes, and regulations. Today, online commercial databases, especially LexisNexis and Westlaw, dominate the legal research field. Additionally, legal researchers today rely on free web resources, search engines, blogs, and wikis. But print resources remain relevant for a number of reasons.

One reason to be familiar with print tools is that many online tools are based on them, and it is difficult to understand how to use online research tools without first understanding how print sources structure legal information. Moreover, some research tasks can still be accomplished more efficiently in print. For example, searching in print may be preferable when you are establishing general knowledge or exploring complex concepts; when you do not yet have a solid grasp of relevant search terms; or when you are doing historical research and the materials are not online. Also, in some situations, you may have limited access to commercial databases. On the other hand, searching online may be preferable when you are looking for unique search terms or fact situations; when the question can be narrowly drawn or involves an emerging area of law; or when time is a consideration. Online research also simplifies time-intensive tasks like 50-state surveys.

Another reason to consult print sources is that they may be the only authentic versions of the law. Many courts, legislatures, and administrative agencies publish primary law online (such as court decisions, legislation, regulations, or administrative decisions), but not all online documents are considered "official" or authentic.[1] Check for disclaimers to determine the location of the official document. For example, the disclaimer on the Washington State Courts Opinions page, www.courts.wa.gov/opinions, reads, "This database contains slip opinions. Slip opinions do not necessarily represent the court's final decision in the case since they are subject to reconsideration, modification orders, editorial corrections, and withdrawal. The official reports advance sheets and bound volumes supersede the slip opinions on this site."

---

1. The shift from print to digital publication has increased access to legal information but also raised issues about authentication of official publications. In 2007, the National Conference of Commissioners on Uniform State Laws approved the creation of a Study Committee on Online Authentication of Legal Materials to discuss the feasibility of a uniform law or model act on digital authentication.

Still, the tendency today for most new researchers is to operate in an online environment. Most students entering law school today are digital natives who have grown up with technology such as computers, cell phones, and MP3 players. But many law professors, judges, and senior attorneys learned legal research when print sources dominated, and they are highly skilled using print tools. Now, however, even very senior legal researchers have learned the advantages of online tools; newer researchers would do well to learn the advantages of print as well. Regardless of your approach, efficient and cost-effective legal research generally requires the use of both print and online resources.

Reading this book will help you develop skills using particular tools and sources but, at a fundamental level, you should *focus on core tasks* (e.g., "I need to find cases on this issue") *rather than on particular tools* (e.g., "I need to use a digest" or "I need to search on LexisNexis"). During your legal career, the tools that you use for a given tasks will change—either because some tools disappear and others are created, or simply because your preferences change—but you will always need to think in terms of core tasks.

III. Key Research Tools

A legal researcher can increase the chances of finding relevant material by using highly regarded and dependable research tools. The following section describes a number of established, reputable online legal research sites.

A. Commercial Databases

LexisNexis and Westlaw are the largest commercial providers of legal information.[2] Both have reputations for accurate material and user-friendly search techniques. Both provide extensive coverage of

---

2. Westlaw is the online service of West, a Thomson Reuters business. The LexisNexis service is part of the LexisNexis Group, a division of Reed Elsevier PLC.

primary and secondary authority. But particular sources available on LexisNexis and Westlaw vary because each company's databases are based, in part, on proprietary print materials. Table 2.1 sets out some of the most important differences in content.

Table 2.1 Differences in Content Between LexisNexis and Westlaw

- LexisNexis and Westlaw both contain federal and state annotated statutes. The depth and breadth of the annotations differ. For example, Westlaw includes as many annotations as possible while LexisNexis is selective, including only the most relevant annotations.

- LexisNexis and Westlaw both contain federal and state cases, but one may contain a particular case that the other does not.

- Differences in secondary sources exist, based on whether the company has acquired the right to include a secondary source in its database. LexisNexis and Westlaw publish certain treatises, formbooks, and other materials, but their coverage is not identical.

- Westlaw has *Washington Practice* (an extensive multivolume treatise focused on Washington law); LexisNexis has a selection of Washington state topical treatises.

- Westlaw has the entire family of *American Jurisprudence* publications (Am Jur 2d, Am Jur Pleading and Practice Forms, Am Jur Legal Forms, Am Jur Trials, Am Jur Proof of Facts), while LexisNexis has *American Jurisprudence 2d* only.

- LexisNexis has *Martindale-Hubbell*, CIS Legislative Histories, Matthew Bender publications, and court records from CourtLink® while Westlaw does not.

- Both LexisNexis and Westlaw have *American Law Reports*. LexisNexis also has Cases in Brief, a product that provides in-depth analysis of selected significant cases and links to secondary sources and news.

- Westlaw contains the West Digest, a topical arrangement of case summaries, while LexisNexis utilizes Search: By Topic or Headnote for the same purpose.

- LexisNexis contains Emerging Issues, commentaries written by experts in the field. The collection includes Practice Insights from all fifty states.

When you sign on to either LexisNexis or Westlaw, you will see jurisdictional or topical tabbed pages that collect the features and databases you use most often. The default tabs in Westlaw vary depending on your type of subscription. The tabs for law school subscribers in Washington State are Law School, Westlaw, Business & News, and Washington. The default tabs in LexisNexis for law school subscribers in Washington State are Legal, News & Business, Public Records, Washington, and Find a Source. The "Washington" tab is a valuable resource, providing shortcuts to the Washington statutes, cases, regulations, forms, directories, secondary sources, journals, news, and more. If your subscription does not automatically provide the Washington tab, create it right away.

Other online commercial providers of legal materials include Loislaw and VersusLaw. They tend to be less expensive than LexisNexis and Westlaw, but they also provide less extensive coverage.

Two free databases, LexisOne and FindLaw, serve as legal information portals, with links to articles, legal news, attorney listings, forms, and recent case law. FindLaw is owned by Thomson Reuters while LexisOne is owned by LexisNexis.

B. Government and Organization Websites

Government entities usually provide free access to information on their websites. These sites generally contain less information than commercial providers, and the search engines on these sites tend to be less sophisticated. But, the depth and breadth of material available on these sites is increasing, making them more useful research tools. Like other states, Washington maintains its own websites for its primary authority. See the Washington State government portal, "Access Washington," at http://access.wa.gov. Although the print versions are the "official" authority, the online versions can be useful for research. The main limitation to these sites is that only recent material may be available.

Another free online source of legal information is the research website maintained by the Municipal Research & Services Center

(MRSC). MRSC is a non-profit, independent organization that provides services to city and county governments in Washington. MRSC's regular website is one of the most comprehensive local government sites in the United States, and its research website has a searchable database of primary authority.

C. University Websites

A number of universities and law schools maintain websites that provide reliable, though limited, information. In Washington, the law libraries at Gonzaga University, Seattle University, and the University of Washington all maintain websites containing Washington legal materials and links to other relevant websites. Each law library also provides legal research guides highlighting key resources and research methods for a particular area of law.

Table 2.2 sets out selected legal research websites.

Table 2.2 Selected Legal Research Websites

Commercial Websites	
LexisNexis	www.lexis.com
Westlaw	www.westlaw.com
Loislaw	www.loislaw.com
VersusLaw	www.versuslaw.com
FindLaw	www.findlaw.com
LexisOne	www.lexisone.com
Government Websites	
State of Washington	http://access.wa.gov
MRSC (Municipal Research & Services Center) Legal Research	www.legalWA.org
University Websites	
Gonzaga University Chastek Law Library	www.law.gonzaga.edu/library
Seattle University Law Library	www.law.seattleu.edu/library.html
University of Washington Gallagher Law Library	http://lib.law.washington.edu

IV. LexisNexis and Westlaw Fundamentals

As noted, online sources play an increasingly important role in legal practice. Indeed, the number of electronic sources can overwhelm a novice researcher. For that reason, this book focuses on how to find information using LexisNexis, Westlaw, and a few key legal research tools provided by government sources. This book concentrates on basic technique—it does not attempt to address all the different ways to access the same information on these services. Training material available on both LexisNexis and Westlaw can introduce you to these possibilities.[3]

Below, the chapter discusses how to retrieve documents when you have a citation and then addresses three specific search methods: "table of contents searching," "terms and connectors searching," and "natural language searching." Although these explanations refer to LexisNexis and Westlaw, they can be applied to other online sources.

A. Beginning Research with a Citation

When you have a citation to a case, statute, article, or other legal source, retrieving that document online is as simple as typing the citation into a designated box on the proper screen. On LexisNexis, click on "Get a Document" and type in the citation. On Westlaw, type the citation into the "Find by citation" box that appears in the left frame. Each service also allows you to retrieve cases by party name.

When you have a citation, you can also start your research by using a *citator* (Shepard's on LexisNexis and KeyCite on Westlaw). Citators are tools that allow you to retrieve all the documents that have referred to your source. For additional information about citators, see Chapter 7.

---

3. For research assistance, call LexisNexis at (800) 455-3947 and Westlaw at (800) 733-2889.

B. Table of Contents Searching

If you do not have a citation, a source's table of contents is often the best place to begin your research. Table of contents searching has several advantages. Unlike searching the full text of a document, searching a table of contents allows you to look for general concepts, not just specific words. This kind of conceptual searching can be particularly helpful early in the research process. In addition, online tables of contents are usually "expandable": by clicking on a "+" sign to the left of an entry, you can see what subentries are contained within the entry. This expansion allows you to see the relationship between concepts and get a good sense of the overall content of a source, a perspective you generally cannot achieve with terms and connectors searching. Finally, the results of table of contents searching are more organized and more closely resemble the results of print research—features that can help you learn more about the field in which you are researching and guard against information overload.

Not every source has a table of contents you can search online. But both Westlaw and LexisNexis provide easy access to tables of contents for many important online sources. On Westlaw, for example, if you want to find the table of contents for state statutes, you can click on the Law School tab and then on the "Statutes by State" database. On the next screen, you will see a list of state codes and, next to each of them, a link to its table of contents. Similarly, on LexisNexis, you can find the table of contents for state statutes by clicking first on "States Legal—U.S.," which you can find under the Legal tab. Once you select the state you are interested in researching, you can click on the statutory code for that state. An expandable table of contents appears automatically. It is also possible to access tables of contents for sources on Westlaw and LexisNexis in other ways. The best approach is often to click on the source you wish to use and to examine the screen for ways to access the table of contents.

C. Terms and Connectors Searching

One of the strengths of doing legal research online is that it allows you to use *terms and connectors* searching. Terms and connectors searches look for particular words in some defined proximity to each other in the full text of a document. Doing these searches on LexisNexis and Westlaw is similar to doing them with a general online search engine such as Google, but it is a bit more complex because you need to choose a database (the collection of documents in which you would like to search). Also, when doing full text searches on LexisNexis and Westlaw, you need to be thoughtful about your choice of search terms and your use of connectors between search terms.

1. Selecting a Database

Unlike a search on a general search engine, a search on LexisNexis or Westlaw requires you to begin by choosing a subset of the site's resources. LexisNexis and Westlaw divide their vast resources into groups by jurisdiction, topic, and type of document. On LexisNexis, these groups are called "sources"; on Westlaw, information is grouped into "databases" (for simplicity, and in order to prevent confusion with print "sources," this book refers to the subgroups on both sites as "databases").

Each chapter in this book helps you choose a database in which to run searches. However, there are a few basic points to keep in mind. First, you can learn about the content of a particular source or database, by clicking on the "i" next to the name of the source or database in either LexisNexis or Westlaw.

Second, the same set of documents often appears in more than one database. For this reason, it is often advantageous to limit your search to the smallest database that will contain the documents you need. Smaller databases will produce a more focused set of results and also tend to be less expensive to access than their larger counterparts. For example, on both LexisNexis and Westlaw, you can search a database that has cases from all of the state and federal courts in the country. (These databases, however, include a premium surcharge.) You can also search a database that has cases just from courts in Washington. Both databases will have cases from the Washington Supreme Court. If you are doing research on an issue of Washington law, you do not want to waste time and money running a search in a database with cases from the entire country.

2. Generating Search Terms

At the beginning of your project you should develop a comprehensive list of *research terms*, which can be legal terms or words that describe your client's situation. Developing such a list requires brainstorming. Some researchers ask the journalistic questions: Who? What? How? Why? When? Where? Others use a mnemonic device like TARPP, which stands for Things, Actions, Remedies, People, and Places.[4] Whether you use one of these suggestions or develop your own method, your goal is to generate a broad range of research terms regarding the facts of your client's situation, the issues involved, and the desired solutions. Try to think of synonyms and antonyms for each term to expand your list. Both Westlaw and LexisNexis incorporate a thesaurus into their search tools to facilitate this process.

For example, suppose you are a defense attorney who was recently assigned to a burglary case. Around midnight, your client allegedly used a piece of wood to break a window at a stereo store, where she stole $2,000 worth of equipment. She was charged with first-degree burglary. Under the relevant statute, a person commits first-degree burglary if he or she is "armed with a deadly weapon." You must determine whether there is a good argument for dismissing the charge based on the fact that the only weapon your client had was the piece of wood she used as a burglar tool. Table 2.3 provides examples of research terms you might use to begin work on this project.

As your research progresses, you will discover new search terms to include in the list. For example, you may read cases that give you insights into the key words judges tend to use in discussing this topic. Or you may learn a *term of art*, a word or phrase that has special meaning in a particular area of law. Add these key words and terms of art to your list.

---

4. *See also* Steven M. Barkan, Roy M. Mersky & Donald J. Dunn, *Fundamentals of Legal Research* 15 (9th ed. 2009) (explaining "TARP," a similar mnemonic device).

Table 2.3 Generating Research Terms

Journalistic Approach	
Who:	Thief, robber, burglar, business owner, property owner
What:	Burglary, crime, first degree, second degree, weapon
How:	Armed, breaking and entering, burglar tools, trespassing
Why:	Theft, stealing, stolen goods
When:	Midnight
Where:	Store, building, commercial establishment, business, shop
TARPP Approach	
Things:	Burglar tool, stolen goods, deadly weapon
Actions:	Burglary, breaking and entering, trespassing, damages, crime
Remedies:	First degree, second degree, incarceration
People:	Thief, robber, burglar, business owner, property owner
Places:	Store, building, commercial establishment, business, shop

3. Constructing a Terms and Connectors Query

Although LexisNexis and Westlaw allow you to conduct a search by typing in a single word, searching with a single word will most likely generate too many documents. For this reason, you need to add more terms and connect them using logical connectors.

a. Using Boolean Connectors

The most effective searches usually result from combining terms using Boolean[5] connectors. These connectors enable you to set search parameters limiting your results to documents that contain certain sets of phrases or word combinations. To use Boolean con-

---

5. George Boole was a British mathematician. The Boolean connectors that carry his name dictate the logical relationship of search terms to each other.

nectors effectively, think of the ideal document you would like to find and try to imagine where your search terms would be located in relationship to each other in that document. Would they be used within a few words of each other? In the same sentence? The same paragraph? Then construct a search that will retrieve only those documents.

For example, suppose your supervisor asked you to research whether a covenant not to compete in an employment contract was invalid because it was a restraint of trade. You might come up with search terms such as *employer, employee, covenant, contract, compete, competition, noncompetition,* and *restraint of trade.* You could create the following search: *employ! /p (covenant or contract) /p (noncompetition or compet!) /p "restraint of trade."* The computer will look for a document with these terms in a rather specific placement:

- Variations of *employ, employee, employer,* and *employment*
- Within the same paragraph as either the term *covenant* or the term *contract*
- And also in that same paragraph, the term *noncompetition* or variations of *competition, compete,* and *competitor*
- And finally, also in that paragraph, the phrase *"restraint of trade."*

Table 2.4 sets out sample Boolean connectors and commands.

Overall, Westlaw and LexisNexis use similar Boolean connectors, and the same search techniques generally work well on both systems. The key differences in the LexisNexis and Westlaw search language are as follows:

1. LexisNexis assumes a blank space signals a phrase, but Westlaw assumes "or." If you type in: *restraint of trade* on LexisNexis, it will look for the phrase; Westlaw will look for: *"restraint"* or *"of"* or *"trade."* Westlaw will read something as a phrase only if you put it in quotes, *"restraint of trade."*

2. LexisNexis and Westlaw use different indicators for segment searches. Example, for case name: LexisNexis: *name(lawrence and texas)*; Westlaw: *ti(lawrence and texas).*

Table 2.4 Boolean Connectors and Commands

Goal	LexisNexis	Westlaw
Search terms as a phrase	Adjacent words default as a phrase: *covenant not to compete*	Quotation marks required: *"covenant not to compete"*
Find either term anywhere in the document	or *compete or noncompetition*	space (or use "or") *compete noncompetition*
Find both terms anywhere in the document	and *restraint and trade*	and *restraint and trade*
Word must appear at least x number of times	atleast *atleast10(noncompetition)*	atleast (or use the button for "term frequency") *atleast10(noncompetition)*
Find two words in the same document within a specified number of words of each other	w/n (or /n) *covenant w/2 noncompet!*	/n *covenant w/2 noncompet!*
Find words in the same sentence	w/s (or /s) *employee /s covenant*	/s *employee /s covenant*
Find words in the same paragraph	w/p (or /p) *employee /p noncompet!*	/p *employee /p noncompet!*
Exclude the second search term	and not *restraint and not prior*	% (or "but not") *restraint % prior*
Universal character	* *Anders*n =Andersen or Anderson*	* *Anders*n =Andersen or Anderson*
Truncation	! *compet! = compete, competition, competent, etc.*	! *compet! = compete, competition, competent, etc.*
Hyphenated words	hyphen read as a space, so hyphenated word is seen as two words *pre-trial = pre-trial or pre trial,* but not *pretrial*	use hyphenated form to retrieve all variations: *pre-trial = pre-trial, pre trial, pretrial*

3. LexisNexis does not allow using /n in the same search as /s or /p, but Westlaw does. Example: *pay /3 equity /s Washington*—Westlaw allows this search, but LexisNexis does not.

b. Expanding or Restricting Your Results

As the previous example makes clear, effective searching with terms and connectors can be complex. Many of your initial searches will locate either no documents or more than 1,000 documents, results that are not helpful. If this happens, do not give up. With practice, you will learn to craft more precise searches that produce more helpful results.

Sometimes a beginning researcher will construct a terms and connectors search that has so many connectors and such specific requirements that it produces no results at all. If this happens, use broader connectors (e.g., search for terms in the same paragraph rather than in the same sentence) or use different terms.

The opposite problem occurs if you do not include enough requirements or your connectors are too broad. If your search produces a long list of results, skim them to see whether they are on point. If many of the results seem irrelevant, modify or edit your search by omitting broad terms or using narrower connectors.

Another way to narrow your results is to use the "Focus" feature on LexisNexis or the "Locate" feature on Westlaw. These features allow you to construct a search within a search and produce a subset of the initial search result. Using these features can save money by avoiding additional charges for a new search.

c. Increasing Precision Using Segments and Fields

Many online legal research websites, including LexisNexis and Westlaw, allow you to search specific parts of documents such as the sections including the date, author, or court. On LexisNexis these specific parts are called document "segments"; on Westlaw they are called "fields."

When you enter the search screens for LexisNexis and Westlaw, you have the option to add segment and field restrictions. You can add these field restrictions onto a basic terms and connectors search. For example, you could run the employment contract search above and add a segment or field to restrict the search to opinions written by a certain judge.[6]

C. Natural Language Searching

LexisNexis and Westlaw allow a second kind of term searching called *natural language searching*. In a natural language search, you simply type in a question or a list of words and let the research software decide which words are critical, whether the words should appear in some proximity to one another, and how often they appear in the document.

Natural language searching tends to be imprecise and is unlikely to produce an exhaustive list of relevant authorities. Nevertheless, some researchers use natural language searching early in their research, skimming through the results quickly to see if there is "one good case," which they can then use to find other relevant sources. Because this hit and miss approach is often not efficient and does not build sophisticated research or analytical skills, this book does not cover natural language searching in depth.

---

6. You can also run segment or field searches by themselves (without any additional terms and connectors). For example, you could search for opinions on any topic written by a certain judge.

Chapter 3

Secondary Sources

Other legal professionals have already researched and analyzed many of the issues you will face in law practice and have published their results in legal encyclopedias, treatises, law review articles, practice guides, and other *secondary sources*. These sources are *secondary* because they provide commentary on cases, statutes, and other primary authority.

Secondary sources are often the best place to begin a research project. These sources introduce you to important background information and help you better comprehend the legal issue you are researching. For example, a secondary source will likely explain unfamiliar terminology and concepts and help you develop an effective list of research terms. Secondary sources will also help you understand the statutes and cases when you read them. Finally, they provide important research leads, often citing key cases, statutes, and rules.

This chapter introduces the most commonly used secondary sources and explains how to use them. The process for using secondary sources varies depending on the source. A general outline is provided in Table 3.1.

I. Legal Encyclopedias

Like other encyclopedias you may be familiar with, legal encyclopedias provide general information on a wide variety of subjects. Legal encyclopedias are organized by subject matter under *topics*, which are presented alphabetically. There are two national legal encyclopedias, and Washington has two state-specific encyclopedic

Table 3.1 Outline for Researching Secondary Sources

1.	Generate a list of research terms.
2.	Search the library's catalog or an online directory for relevant sources.
3.	Search the index of a secondary source (print only), browse the table of contents, or run a terms and connectors search (online only).
4.	Find the relevant portion in the main volumes (print) or link to the relevant portion (online). Reading the commentary will assist your comprehension of the legal issues. Within the commentary, often in footnotes, you will find references to primary authority.
5.	Update the secondary source, if possible.
6.	Read the primary authority.

sources. When you are researching an issue governed by state law, one of the best places to start your research is with one of these Washington sources.

A. *Washington Practice*

Washington Practice, a West series, is one of Washington's state-specific, encyclopedic sources and is available in print and online through Westlaw (WAPRAC). It has more than two dozen titles that cover topics such as evidence, tort law, and real estate. The titles are listed in Table 3.2 and also appear on Westlaw. Almost all the titles take up more than one volume. Each volume contains a table of contents specific to the title contained in that volume. In addition to these volumes, the series includes a main index, which contains key words from all of the volumes.

The *Washington Practice* titles fall into different categories and serve different functions. For example, the first title, "Methods of Practice," has relatively short entries on many topics, some of which are covered in more depth in other titles, along with references for further research. The second title, "Rules Practice," contains the text of the Washington state court rules along with helpful commentary

Table 3.2 Titles in *Washington Practice*
(in approximate order titles appear within the set)

Methods of Practice
Rules Practice
Evidence
Courtroom Handbook on Washington Evidence
Washington Pattern Jury Instructions—Civil
Uniform Commercial Code Forms and Commentary
Civil Procedure Forms
Washington Pattern Jury Instructions—Criminal
Criminal Practice and Procedure with Forms
Criminal Law with Sentencing Forms
Civil Procedure
Washington Handbook on Civil Procedure
Tort Law and Practice
Real Estate: Property Law and Transactions
Family and Community Property Law with Forms
Family and Community Property Law Handbook
Environmental Law and Practice
Contract Law and Practice
Elder Law and Practice with Forms
Creditors' Remedies—Debtors' Relief
Motions in Limine
Elements of an Action
DUI Practice Manual
Construction Law Manual
Summary Judgment and Related Motions

---

and case annotations. These annotations are similar to the case descriptions found in an annotated code. Statutes and annotated codes are covered in Chapter 4.

Other titles are classified as "handbooks," one-volume books that are generally intended for use in the courtroom. For example, the evidence handbook contains virtually all Washington statutes affecting the admissibility of evidence (so when a judge asks an attorney "What does the statute say?" the attorney has the information readily available). The evidence handbook contains other useful information as well, such as scripts for the proper phrasing of objections. Similarly, the civil procedure handbook includes nearly all the statutes that affect civil procedure.

The remaining titles, for example "Civil Procedure," "Tort Law and Practice," and "Contract Law and Practice," serve a more general research purpose and contain more detailed analysis of primary legal authority. They often contain the most useful information for legal research and writing projects in law school and internships.

Although *Washington Practice* is available online, many lawyers still prefer the print version because its index and tables of contents are easier to use. To find a topic in print, the first step is generally to look up your research terms in the main index, located in a paperback volume placed at the end of the series. The main index will refer you to the title or titles that address each research term and provide a citation to a chapter and section number. Next, find the volume that contains the title and chapter that addresses each research term. You can determine which volume you need by looking at the volumes' spines, which indicate the title that the volume contains and the range of section numbers within the volume.

Another effective way to find a topic in print is to go directly to the title that relates most closely to your research problem. For example, if your problem involves a question about intentional infliction of emotional distress, you might go directly to the title addressing tort law and practice. Once you find the volumes covering tort law and practice, you will notice that each volume includes a detailed table of contents addressing tort law. If you review this table of contents, you can usually find chapters and sections that pertain to your topic. In addition, the last volume in the each title includes a subject specific index, which is sometimes easier to use than the general index.

Searching *Washington Practice* on Westlaw is also straightforward and, in some respects, mirrors the process used with the print version. The *Washington Practice* series database (WAPRAC) appears under the "Forms, Treatises, CLEs & other Practice Materials" section on the Washington tab. By clicking on this link or typing WAPRAC in the "Search for a Database" box, you will be led to a search screen. This screen includes a "Table of Contents" link near the top of the page. If you click on this link, you can browse the series' expandable table of contents to find relevant titles, chapters, and sections. You can also run a terms and connectors search in WAPRAC. Unfortunately, neither the general nor the title-specific indexes to *Washington Practice* is currently available online.

Whichever research method you choose, be sure to read the relevant material you find before doing additional research. First, skim the introductory material at the beginning of the chapter. This material often provides a good overview of the topic and helps you determine how your research problem fits into the legal landscape. Next, go to the particular section number you found in your research, and read the entry pertaining to your topic. Pay particularly close attention to the footnotes, which often cite to pivotal cases and statutes and allow you to identify very quickly the main primary authority that you will need to analyze your problem.

In addition to pointing directly to key primary sources, *Washington Practice* contains references to relevant topic and key numbers used in West's Digests, along with citations to other West publications. As you will see in Chapter 6, these topics and key numbers allow you to identify cases that pertain to the issue that you are researching. Figure 3.1 contains an excerpt from the text and footnotes of a *Washington Practice* section.

As with any source, the last step in using *Washington Practice* is to update what you have found. The print version of *Washington Practice* is updated with a pocket part (and occasionally a supplement), so make sure to check the back of the book for newer information. The online version of *Washington Practice* is current through the most recently revised print edition or pocket part.

B. *Washington Lawyers Practice Manual*

The other Washington-specific encyclopedic source is the *Washington Lawyers Practice Manual* (WLPM), which is published by the King County Bar Association. It is in loose-leaf form (in eight three-ring binders) and is not available online. It is also available on CD-ROM, which some law firms use.

Figure 3.1 Excerpt from *Washington Practice*
Real Estate: Property Law

Chapter 8 Adverse Possession and Related Doctrines

§ 8.9 Actual Possession — Principles

To be adverse, the possession of another's land must be "actual": it is not possible to be in adverse possession without physical occupation. Unless there is the requisite degree of physical possession, no amount of verbal claims, no amount of documents, no kind of acts off the ground will put the claimant in adverse possession.[1] Paying taxes on someone else's land is not possession, nor is filing a plat that includes it, nor suing for possession of it, nor even giving the owner express notice that you claim title.[2] Having a community reputation as the owner does not constitute possession.[3]

[1] *See Snively v. State*, 167 Wash. 385, 9 P.2d 773 (1932) (state's claim that lake was navigable did not put state in possession of it); *Cartwright v. Hamilton*, 111 Wash. 685, 191 P. 797 (1920) (maintaining fence on neighbor's land not possession without use up to fence).

[2] *Booten v. Peterson*, 34 Wn. 2d 563, 209 P.2d 349 (1949) (express claim); *Loose v. Locke*, 25 Wn. 2d 599, 171 P.2d 849 (1946) (paying taxes); *Ferry v. Hodson*, 22 Wn. 2d 613, 156 P.2d 913 (1945) (plat; bringing suit); *Austrian American Benevolent Cemetery Ass'n v. Desrochers*, 124 Wash. 179, 214 P. 3 (1923), *affirmed on rehearing* 124 Wash. 179, 216 P. 891 (1923) (paying taxes).

[3] *McInerney v. Beck*, 10 Wash. 515, 39 P. 130 (1895).

Source: *Washington Practice*, William B. Stoebuck & John W. Weaver, Real Estate: Property Law, § 8.9. Reprinted with permission of West, a Thomson Reuters business.

The manual has twenty-two chapters, each covering a frequently used area of Washington law. For example, chapter titles include "Business Law Practice" and "Real Property Practice." The chapters are written by practicing attorneys, and the information in WLPM is sometimes more practice oriented than the material in *Washington Practice*. In other words, it may contain more detailed information on specific legal procedures (e.g., how to file a certain claim), and it includes many sample forms. Unlike *Washington Practice*, WLPM does not contain footnotes, but it does refer to primary authority throughout the text.

To find information in WLPM, you will first need to go to the appropriate chapter. The spine of each binder indicates which chapters the binder contains. The set does not have an index, but each chapter has a detailed table of contents. Browse the table of contents of relevant chapters to find sections that relate to your search terms. The set is updated with replacement pages, so you do not need to check a pocket part or supplement. Check the cover page of each chapter to see when the chapter was last updated.

C. National Encyclopedias

In addition to the two state-specific encyclopedias, you may also want to use one of the national encyclopedias, *Corpus Juris Secundum* (CJS) and *American Jurisprudence, Second Edition* (Am Jur 2d). National encyclopedias are helpful when you want to know how federal courts or courts in other states treat the issue you are researching. For example, if there is no law on point in Washington or the legal standard is ambiguous, you might need to rely on decisions from other jurisdictions to support your analysis.

To use these encyclopedias in print, first review the softbound index volumes for your research terms. Index entries will include both an abbreviated word or phrase—the topic—and a section number.[1] The encyclopedia's topic abbreviations are explained in tables in the front of the index volumes. Select the bound volume containing a relevant topic. The spine of each volume includes the range of topics included in that volume.

To use national encyclopedias online, you can either browse the encyclopedia's table of contents or do a terms and connectors search. The table of contents for both encyclopedias is long and detailed, so you may need to look under several topics before finding one on point. On Westlaw, both encyclopedias are listed under "Treatises,

---

1. Do not confuse these topics and section numbers with the West digest system of topics and key numbers discussed in Chapter 6.

CLEs, Practice Guides" in the directory. On LexisNexis, Am Jur 2d is linked under "Secondary Legal." Note that CJS is not available on LexisNexis.

Once you have found a relevant topic, skim the topical outline at its beginning for an overview. Online, you can use the table of contents feature to see a topical outline; in addition, Westlaw allows you to link to "Topic Contents" and sometimes a "Topic Summary" from within individual sections. Once you have an overview of the topic, link to the particular section number and read the relevant entries. Most encyclopedia entries are cursory because the goal of the writers is to summarize the law. Encyclopedia entries will identify any variations that exist among the different jurisdictions, but they do not attempt to resolve differences or recommend improvements in the law.

Like *Washington Practice*, national encyclopedias include helpful footnotes. The footnotes in CJS and Am Jur 2d cite authorities from all American jurisdictions, and the cases are sometimes not very recent; nevertheless, you can Shepardize or KeyCite (discussed in Chapter 7) an older, relevant case to find more recent authority on point. You can also use the topics and key numbers (discussed in Chapter 6) assigned to a case from another jurisdiction to jump start your research in Washington. In addition, encyclopedias contain references for further research. For example, both CJS and Am Jur 2d cross-reference relevant West topics and key numbers, and Am Jur 2d cross-references *American Law Reports* (discussed below).

II. *American Law Reports*

American Law Reports (ALR) is a hybrid resource, offering both commentary on certain legal subjects and the full text of published cases on those subjects. The commentary articles are called *annotations* (do not confuse these annotations with the case summaries provided as part of the annotations in an unofficial statutory code). ALR annotations tend to focus on very narrow topics, take a practitioner's view, and provide a survey of the law in different jurisdictions. Thus, an annotation on the exact topic of your research is likely to be extremely helpful. Annotations are written by lawyers who are knowledgeable, but not necessarily recognized experts. Each annotation is accompanied by a case that illustrates the point of law discussed in the annotation.

For example: In 1986, Congress passed the *Emergency Medical Treatment and Active Labor Act*, 42 USC § 1395dd (EMTALA). ALR reports a leading EMTALA case, *Thornton v. Southwest Detroit Hospital*, at 104 A.L.R. Fed. 157 (1990) (the standard citation for that case is 895 F.2d 1131 (6th Cir. 1990)). Immediately following the *Thornton* case is an annotation, *Construction and Application of Emergency Medical Treatment and Active Labor Act (42 U.S.C.A. § 1395dd)* at 104 A.L.R. Fed. 166, written by a lawyer named Melissa K. Stull. Among the topics discussed in this annotation are the reasons Congress enacted the EMTALA, the effect of related statutes, the liability imposed on hospitals, and available remedies.

There are several ALR series. Early series contained both state and federal subjects. Currently, federal subjects are included in ALR Federal, now in its second series, while state subjects are discussed in numbered series, ALR 3d through ALR 6th.

To find relevant annotations in the print version of ALR, use one of its indexes. The multivolume ALR Index includes references to annotations in the 2d, 3d, 4th, 5th, 6th, and Fed series. In addition, the one-volume ALR Fed Quick Index is available for finding annotations in the ALR Fed series. A similar one-volume quick index is available for ALR 3d, 4th, 5th, and 6th.

The print version of ALR is updated with pocket parts. You should also check the "Annotation History Table" in the index volumes to see whether an annotation has been supplemented or superseded by another annotation, rather than just updated in pocket parts.

ALR annotations are also available on LexisNexis and Westlaw. Access ALR through the online directory (on LexisNexis, it is under "Secondary Legal"; on Westlaw, it is under "Treatises, CLEs, Practice Guides" and the database identifier is ALR). Although there is no online table of contents, you can run a terms and connectors search to find relevant entries. Another good way to find relevant ALR annotations is to Shepardize or KeyCite a significant case (Shepard's and KeyCite are discussed in Chapter 7). These online citators will list any ALR annotations in which your case is mentioned. Finally, both LexisNexis and Westlaw include citations to ALR and other secondary sources in their "guides on the side": *Results Plus* (Westlaw) and *Practioner's Toolbox* (LexisNexis). These guides appear automatically in a frame next to your search results and suggest other sources to look at.

III. Practice Guides and Continuing Legal Education Publications

Unlike *Washington Practice* and other encyclopedias that cover many areas of law, practice guides focus on a specialized area. These guides explain the current state of the law and include citations to primary materials, sample forms, and practice tips. These guides are often published by state bar associations. Examples in Washington include *Juvenile Criminal Law in Washington: A Practice Guide, Washington Real Property Deskbook, Washington Family Law Deskbook, Washington Appellate Practice Deskbook,* and *Defending DWIs in Washington.*

Another type of publication written with the practicing attorney in mind is *continuing legal education* (CLE) material. The Washington State Bar association requires Washington attorneys to attend CLE courses to maintain their membership. These courses often present practical information on topics ranging from ethical issues in business law to building a personal injury practice. Some CLE courses are aimed at new lawyers just learning the fundamentals of practice; however, many CLE courses offer new insights on cutting-edge legal issues. A CLE course may be led by a practitioner, judge, or law professor, or a group of them. Frequently, the speaker prepares handouts that include sample forms, sample documents, and explanations. These handouts are sometimes bound and published. Unlike practice guides, CLE materials are rarely indexed or typeset (i.e. they may still be in the form of the presenter's handouts).

Although practice guides and CLE materials are probably not of much help in doctrinal classes (e.g., contracts), they are valuable in practice settings. Finding a current practice guide or comprehensive CLE publication that addresses the area of law in which you are researching is often like hitting the research jackpot.

To find a practice guide or CLE publication in print, search the library's catalog by using the phrase "Washington State" and a topic (e.g., "real estate" or "real property") as search terms. Practice guides often have titles that include words such as "handbook," "deskbook," "guide," or "manual." Once you have found a relevant source, use either its index or table of contents to find applicable sections.

Many Washington practice guides are in loose-leaf (binder) form, and they are updated with replacement pages (so you do not have to look in a pocket part). CLE materials are not usually updated; instead, newer materials appear and completely replace older ones. Sometimes the updates are not integrated; look for colored pages supplementing a chapter. Always check the date of publication for practice guides and CLE materials. Although older material can still be useful, you do not want to spend time reading an outdated source. A good way to know if a source is updated regularly is to see if the copyright date in the catalog is followed by a hyphen (e.g., 1984–), a sign that the library updates the source. In addition, the front of the book may contain colored pages indicating when the book was last updated.

Fewer practice guides and CLE materials are available online than in print. LexisNexis has some Washington-specific practice material; available titles are linked to "Search Analysis and CLE Materials" under your Washington tab. A more comprehensive online source for Washington practice materials is Loislaw (www.loislaw.com). Loislaw includes a complete set of Washington State Bar Association deskbooks and CLE materials on various topics, including estate planning, family law, real estate, alternative dispute resolution, ethics, and general practice. These useful resources are not available on LexisNexis or Westlaw.

You can also find practice guides and CLE materials for issues involving federal law (e.g., *The Corporate Counsel's Guide to the Family and Medical Leave Act).* Locate these materials in print using the library catalog just as you would find state materials (but use the phrase "United States" instead of "Washington State" as a search term). Both LexisNexis and Westlaw have extensive collections of federal practice guides.

IV. Legal Periodicals

A. Law Reviews and Journals

Law reviews and journals publish scholarly articles written by law professors, judges, practitioners, and students. These articles explore specific legal issues in great detail. Freed from the constraints of representing a client's interests or working on a particular case, authors are able to analyze and evaluate the laws currently in force and to propose changes.

Reading articles published in law reviews and journals can provide a thorough understanding of current law, because the authors often explain the existing law before making their recommendations. These articles may also identify weaknesses or new trends in the law that affect your client's situation. The many footnotes in law review and law journal articles often provide excellent summaries of relevant research.

Articles written by students are called "Notes" or "Comments." Although not as authoritative as articles written by recognized experts, student articles often provide clear and careful analysis, and their footnotes are valuable research tools. Students also write shorter law review pieces called "Case Notes" or "Recent Developments." These pieces notify readers of important developments in the law but do not analyze or critique the law in much depth.

Law reviews and law journals are generally edited by law students who were selected according to academic performance or through a writing competition. Most law reviews have general audiences and cover a broad range of topics. The most well known examples include the *Harvard Law Review,* the *Yale Law Journal,* and the *Stan-*

Table 3.3 Law Reviews and Journals Published by
Washington Law Schools

Across Borders: The Gonzaga Journal of International Law (electronic publication only) — Gonzaga University School of Law

Gonzaga Law Review — Gonzaga University School of Law

Pacific Rim Law and Policy Journal — University of Washington School of Law

Seattle Journal for Social Justice — Seattle University School of Law

Seattle University Law Review — Seattle University School of Law

Shidler Journal for Law, Commerce & Technology (electronic publication only) — University of Washington School of Law

Washington Law Review — University of Washington School of Law

---

ford Law Review. Other law journals focus on a specific area of law, for example the *Seattle Journal for Social Justice*, the *Journal of Environmental Law and Litigation*, and the *Columbia Journal of Transactional Law*. Still other law journals are "peer edited," meaning that law professors select and edit the articles to be published. Some well known examples include: *Constitutional Commentary*; the *Journal of Law and Economics*; *Law, Culture and the Humanities*; and the *Journal of Legal Education*.

When researching an issue involving Washington law, you may want to look for articles in journals published by law schools in Washington. These journals are more likely than journals published elsewhere to contain articles addressing Washington law. But keep in mind that some legal issues in Washington receive national attention and generate articles in other law reviews. Table 3.3 lists the law reviews published by Washington law schools.

Most law reviews and journals are published first in soft-cover booklets. Later, several issues will be bound into a single volume. Articles are cited by volume number, the name of the journal, and the first page of the article. Articles are not updated in the usual sense, but you can find other articles that have cited any given article by using Shepard's or KeyCite (discussed in Chapter 7).

B. Bar Journals

Each state's bar journal contains articles of particular interest to attorneys practicing in that state. In addition, the American Bar Association publishes the *ABA Journal*, which has articles of general interest to attorneys across the nation. The *ABA Journal* is available on both LexisNexis (ABAJNL) and on Westlaw (ABAJ).

Articles in bar journals are often shorter and more sparsely footnoted than law review articles. Bar journal articles tend to have a practitioner's focus. For example, the *Washington State Bar News* frequently contains articles on trends in law practice and firm management and articles analyzing recent changes in the law. While the *Washington State Bar News* is currently not included on LexisNexis or Westlaw, articles are available at www.wsba.org. Local bar associations may also publish journals or newsletters.

C. Locating Law Review or Bar Journal Articles

There are two indexes you can use to find legal periodicals: the *Index to Legal Periodicals and Books* (ILPB) and the *Current Law Index* (CLI).[2] Although these indexes are available in print, it is much easier to access them electronically. They are both available on Westlaw and LexisNexis, although the online version of CLI is called the "Legal Resource Index" (LRI). Your law library may also subscribe to an online version of CLI (accessible through the library's catalog) called "LegalTrac" or an online version of ILPB called "Wilsonline." You may have an easier time finding articles in one of the versions of the CLI

---

2. ILPB and CLI are periodical indexes. They do not index a particular source but provide citations to articles found in law reviews, journals, and legal newspapers.

because its headings are more specific than those used in the ILPB and it covers more publications.

You can also search full-text databases of journals and law reviews on LexisNexis or Westlaw. For increased efficiency, you may want to restrict searches to specific journals, topics, or jurisdictions.

V. Treatises and Other Books

In addition to practice guides, other publications provide a more in-depth discussion than is usually found in an encyclopedia entry. These include treatises, hornbooks, and *Nutshells*. All of these publications cover a particular legal subject, such as contracts or civil procedure, but differ in their level of coverage. Treatises are generally more comprehensive than hornbooks, which offer a more summarized view. *Nutshells* offer an even more condensed explanation of law than hornbooks. Accordingly, an attorney may use a treatise to become familiar with a new area of law, while a law student might turn to a hornbook or *Nutshell* to prepare for class or to better understand a class lecture.

Some treatises are so well known and widely respected that a colleague or supervisor may suggest that you begin research with a particular title. Examples include *Corbin on Contracts*; *Nimmer on Copyright*; Wright & Miller's *Federal Practice and Procedure*; and Moore's *Federal Practice*. These can be either one-volume or multivolume treatises. Many are available online but only on the commercial service affiliated with their publisher. Figure 3.2 provides a sample page from a well known treatise.

You can locate treatises, hornbooks, and *Nutshells* in print by using a library's catalog and searching for the general subject matter of your research project. After finding one book on point, scan the other titles shelved around it for additional resources.

After locating a relevant book, begin with either the table of contents or the index. In multivolume treatises, the index is often in the last volume. Locate your research terms and record the references given. The

Figure 3.2 Excerpt from Wright & Miller's *Federal Practice and Procedure*

GENERAL FEDERAL QUESTION JURISDICTION

3561.   Federal Question Jurisdiction—In General.
3561.1   Amount in Controversy.
3562.   The Meaning of "Arising Under."
3563.   "Constitution, Laws, or Treaties of the United States."
3564.   Substantiality of the Federal Question.
3565.   "Protective Jurisdiction."
3566.   Determination From the Well-Pleaded Complaint.

§ 3561. Federal Question Jurisdiction—In General

The Constitution provides that federal courts may be given jurisdiction over "Cases, in Law and Equity, arising under this Constitution, the Laws of the United States, and Treaties made, or which shall be made, under their authority." [1] Cases falling within this provision are usually said to invoke "federal question" [2] jurisdiction or, occasionally, "arising under" jurisdiction. [3]

[1] **Constitution**
U.S. Const., Art. III, § 2

[2] **"Federal question"**
Empire Healthchoice Assur., Inc. v. McVeigh, 547 U.S. 677, 126 S. Ct. 2121, 2131, 165 L. Ed. 2d 131 (2006).
Grable & Sons Metal Products, Inc. v. Darue Engineering & Mfg., 545 U.S. 308, 312, 125 S. Ct. 2363, 2366, 162 L. Ed. 2d 257 (2005).
Merrell Dow Pharmaceuticals Inc. v. Thompson, 478 U.S. 804, 807, 106 S. Ct. 3229, 3232, 92 L. Ed. 2d 650 (1986).
National Farmers Union Ins. Companies v. Crow Tribe of Indians, 471 U.S. 845, 853, 105 S. Ct. 2447, 2452, 85 L. Ed. 2d 818 (1985).
Thurston Motor Lines, Inc. v. Jordan K. Rand, Ltd., 460 U.S. 533, 535, 103 S. Ct. 1343, 1344, 75 L. Ed. 2d 260 (1983).
Steffel v. Thompson, 415 U.S. 452, 464, 94 S. Ct. 1209, 1218, 39 L. Ed. 2d 505 (1974).
Oneida Indian Nation of N.Y. State v. Oneida County, New York, 414 U.S. 661, 94 S. Ct. 772, 776, 785, 39 L. Ed. 2d 73 (1974).

Figure 3.2 Excerpt from Wright & Miller's
Federal Practice and Procedure, continued

See also
American Law Institute, Federal Judicial Code Revision Project, published in an appendix of Volume 19A of this treatise.
American Law Institute, Study of Division of Jurisdiction between State and Federal Courts, Official Draft, 1969, p. 162.

[3] "Arising under" jurisdiction
Empire Healthchoice Assur., Inc. v. McVeigh, 547 U.S. 677, 126 S. Ct. 2121, 2141, 165 L. Ed. 2d 131 (2006).
Grable & Sons Metal Products, Inc. v. Darue Engineering & Mfg., 545 U.S. 308, 312, 125 S. Ct. 2363, 2366, 162 L. Ed. 2d 257 (2005).

Source: 13D Charles Alan Wright et al., *Federal Practice and Procedure* § 3561 (3d ed. 2009). Reprinted with permission of West, a Thomson Reuters business.

reference will be to a page number, section number, or paragraph number, depending on the publisher. Turn to that part of the book, read the text, and note any pertinent primary authority cited in the footnotes.

Print treatises are updated in a variety of ways. Bound volumes like *Corbin on Contracts* and *Federal Practice and Procedure* are updated with pocket parts. Still others are updated with pocket parts and then with subsequent editions. Moore's *Federal Practice* is published in loose-leaf binders, which are updated by replacing outdated pages throughout the binder with current material. Each page is dated to show when it was last updated. Also, colored pages at the beginning of loose-leaf binders are sometimes used to indicate when the binder was last updated. *Nutshells* are published in later editions much more frequently than treatises or hornbooks.

Online, you can find numerous treatises on LexisNexis and Westlaw, although neither service generally contains student-oriented hornbooks or *Nutshells*. You can locate relevant treatises on Westlaw by looking in the directory under "Forms, Treatises, CLEs, and Other Practice Materials" or your general topic (e.g., "Corporations"). On LexisNexis, you can locate relevant treatises by looking under "Secondary Legal" under the Legal Tab or by choosing your general topic.

Once you find a relevant treatise online, you can use a terms and connectors search to locate pertinent sections. However, it is often more helpful to scan the treatise's table of contents to get an overview of the topic and to see neighboring sections that may also be relevant. LexisNexis displays the table of contents on the initial screen for each secondary source. In addition to searching the full text of the source, you can search the table of contents only. Westlaw provides a link to the table of contents at the top of the screen.

Online treatises are generally at least as up to date as the latest pocket parts of their print versions. Clicking on the "i" next to the name of the treatise provides the date through which the material is current.

VI. Forms

Forms may be used in legal research to help draft legal documents, such as a petition or complaint, or transactional matters such as a buy-sell agreement. Many formbook series and practice treatises offer drafting advice in addition to sample forms. For example, *Washington Practice* integrates legal forms within topical chapters. In advising a client on petitioning for a name change, you might look at *Washington Practice, Methods of Practice* § 23.5 for an explanation of the process and § 25.11 for a sample petition. Or in drafting a buy-sell agreement, you might look at *Washington Practice, Methods of Practice* § 73.70 for a sample asset purchase agreement. When you use forms, it is critical that you understand each word in the sample and modify it to suit your client's needs. Do not simply fill in the blanks.

Treatises, practice manuals, and CLE materials often include relevant forms. To identify these materials, search the library's catalog under the subject you want. Books that have a lot of forms are cataloged with the subheadings "forms" in the subject heading, for instance: Trial Practice—Washington (State)—Forms.

Forms are available in many sources. The Washington Courts website (www.courts.wa.gov) includes a number of family law forms and other forms dealing with criminal law, garnishment, name change, and small claims. The Washington LawHelp website (www.washingtonlawhelp.org) has forms on a wide variety of legal issues, including consumer law, family law, and housing law. Most of the forms are written by lawyers at the Northwest Justice Project or other nonprofit groups. Many of them are translated into other languages. Formbooks are also available on Lexis-Nexis and Westlaw. Look under your particular topic in the online directory to see the related formbooks. On Westlaw, you can also locate formbooks by looking under the heading "Forms, Treatises, CLEs, and Other Practice Materials."

VII. Loose-leaf Services

A loose-leaf service combines both primary and secondary sources under one title. A single loose-leaf service may contain statutes, administrative regulations, annotations to cases and agency opinions, and commentary. The benefit is that all of the material is gathered together so that you do not have to consult multiple sources. Examples of two widely used loose-leafs are the *Standard Federal Tax Reporter* and the *Family Law Reporter*.

A. Loose-leafs in Print

These mini-libraries of primary and secondary sources are called "loose-leaf services" because the pages are kept in loose-leaf notebooks instead of being bound as books. Major publishers include the Bureau of National Affairs (BNA), Commerce Clearing House (CCH), Matthew Bender, and Research Institute of America (RIA). The loose-leaf format allows the publisher to send updates frequently and quickly; the outdated pages are removed and the new pages inserted on a regular basis. A loose-leaf service generally fills many volumes, which may be arranged by topic, or by statute, or using another system.

Loose-leaf services always have a "How to Use" section, generally near the beginning of the first volume. You should review this section before starting your research. You may also want to skim through a few volumes to become familiar with the organization of that particular service. Pay careful attention to each service's method and frequency of updating.

If you know the section of the loose-leaf that you need to research, you can identify the appropriate volume and turn to the section you need. If you do not know which volume or section you need, it is often best to begin with the topical index, which is often the first or last volume of the series. Look up your research terms, and write down the reference numbers given. These will likely be paragraph numbers rather than page numbers. Even though the page numbers will change with future updates, the paragraph reference will remain constant.

Turn to each paragraph number referenced in the index under your research terms. Realize that the paragraph number may be for the statute, regulations, annotations, or commentary. Turn to earlier and later pages around that paragraph number to ensure that you have reviewed all relevant material.

B. Loose-leafs Online

Many loose-leaf services are also available on LexisNexis and Westlaw. Attorneys — especially in fields like environmental law, labor law, and tax law — rely heavily on loose-leaf services. But access to loose-leaf services online may not be available under all law school subscriptions. If LexisNexis or Westlaw indicates that a particular resource is not available under your subscription, see a reference librarian to explore your options.

VIII. Restatements

A restatement is an organized and detailed summary of the common law in a specific area. Familiar titles include *Restatement of the Law of Contracts* and *Restatement of the Law of Torts*. Restatements are written collaboratively by scholars, practitioners, and judges who are members of American Law Institute (ALI) committees. These committees, led by a scholar called the reporter, draft rules that explain the common law. The committees circulate their drafts for review and revision. The final version of the restatement published by ALI includes not only rules created by the committee but also commentary, illustrations, and the reporter's notes.

Restatements were originally intended simply to summarize the law as it existed, in an effort to build national consistency in key common law areas. Over time, restatements grew more assertive in stating what the authors thought the law should be.

Restatements are secondary authority, but sometimes courts adopt legal interpretations appearing in restatements. If this happens, then the portion of the restatement adopted by the court may be treated as primary authority in that jurisdiction. After a court has adopted a portion of the restatement, the committee's commentary and illustrations, as well as any notes provided by the reporter, may become valuable tools in predicting how courts will apply the restatement's language in future cases.

To find a relevant restatement in print, search the library catalog for the subject matter or search for "restatement." Within each restatement, use the table of contents or index to find pertinent sections. The text of each restatement section is followed by commentary and sometimes illustrations of key points made in the text. Separate "Appendix" volumes list citations to cases that have referred to the restatement (online there may instead be a link to citing cases).

Restatements are available on both LexisNexis and Westlaw. If you access the restatements online, you can use a terms and connectors search, but, as with other sources, browsing the restatement's table of contents is likely to be more helpful.

Restatements themselves are updated only when a later version is published; the Appendix volumes are updated periodically, so be sure to check for a pocket part or supplement and an interim pamphlet. In addition, you can Shepardize or KeyCite a restatement section to find cases or articles that cite the restatement.[3]

---

3. In addition to providing a useful general research tool, restatements may be helpful to students when preparing for class or studying for exams. Many of the hypotheticals used by professors come from the illustrations in restatements.

IX. Uniform Laws and Model Codes

Uniform laws and model codes are written by organizations that hope to harmonize the statutory laws of the fifty states. The most active of these organizations is the National Conference of Commissioners on Uniform State Laws (NCCUSL). Like the ALI, NCCUSL organizes committees of experts to draft uniform laws and model codes. Familiar examples of these secondary sources include the *Uniform Commercial Code* (UCC) and the *Model Penal Code*. Statutory language is drafted, then comments are solicited, and the language is finalized. The published uniform law or model code includes both the proposed statutory language and authors' explanatory notes.

Legislatures sometimes enact uniform laws or model codes, making them primary authority. Other times, legislatures write new statutes, using model codes as a backdrop. In either case, reviewing the explanatory commentary published with these codes can help you understand a statute in your jurisdiction that was based on the uniform or model language. For example, every state has adopted a version of the UCC. In researching Washington's commercial code, you could gain insights from commentary on the UCC that discussed the provisions adopted by Washington. Additionally, cases from other states that have also adopted the same UCC provisions are helpful in interpreting Washington's statute.

Uniform laws and model codes, along with official notes and explanations, are published by the authors. Commercial versions add commentary and often footnotes with case support. West publishes *Uniform Laws Annotated*, which includes an index and research annotations for uniform laws prepared by NCCUSL.

Finding a relevant uniform law or model code is similar to finding a restatement. Search the library catalog for the particular area of law you are researching, such as "criminal law" or "commercial transactions." You may want to include in your search "model code" or "uniform law." In the stacks, scan the titles nearby to determine whether more helpful commercial editions have been published. Within the volume or set of volumes containing the uniform law or model code, look in the table of contents or index.

Uniform laws and model codes are available on LexisNexis and Westlaw. You will find folders with these sources in the directory under "Secondary Legal" (LexisNexis) or "Forms, Treatises, CLEs, and Other Practice Materials" (Westlaw). Many uniform laws and model codes are also included in the digest volume of Martindale-Hubbell, a well-known directory of attorneys (www.martindale.com).

X. Jury Instructions

Jury instructions can be very helpful even if you are only in the early stages of research (e.g., when writing a memo on the probability of success on a claim). Jury instructions tell the jury what each side must prove in order to prevail, and the instructions will often break down a statute or claim into its elements. Jury instructions' summary of legal standards will help you focus your research and better predict the outcome of a given case.

The Washington Supreme Court has a committee on pattern jury instructions for both civil and criminal matters. You can find these instructions in *Washington Practice*. The pattern instructions for civil matters (often referred to as "WPI") are found in volumes 6 and 6A; pattern instructions for criminal matters (often referred to as "WPIC") are found in volumes 11 and 11A. Each set of instructions has an index and table of contents; look up or browse for the name of the action (e.g., burglary) or concept (e.g., reasonable doubt) to find the relevant instructions. Pattern jury instructions are available on Westlaw under the Washington tab (there is no index, but you can access a table of contents). Starting in 2008, Washington pattern jury instructions are available free, as a pilot project, on the courts website (www.courts.wa.gov).

XI. Search Engines and Blogs

A practical secondary source that you should not overlook is a general online search engine such as Google (www.google.com). If you are unfamiliar with an area of law, you can use a search engine to find background information before you look in traditional legal sources. Increasingly, specialized legal materials such as briefs and pleadings are also available online, even when they may not be available through commercial websites.

As you already know, a search in an online search engine can produce hundreds of "hits." One of the best ways to keep your result list more manageable and relevant is to use the search engine's advanced search feature. For example, on Google, you can click on the "Advanced Search Options" link next to the initial search box. From there, you can restrict your results to websites that contain certain phrases or websites that do not contain certain words. You can also restrict your search by domain, e.g. searching only addresses ending in .gov or .org. Another strategy is to use known citations or partial citations in your Google search. For example, if you know that transportation law is in Title 46 of the *Revised Code of Washington* (RCW) and you are looking for the law prohibiting text messaging while driving, search "text and driving and RCW 46."

Legal blogs are an increasingly important source for up-to-date information about pending cases or changes in the law. A particularly well known blog is SCOTUSblog (www.scotusblog.com), which covers the United States Supreme Court, providing summaries of filed cases and oral arguments, confirmation hearings, and more. Several websites, for example Blawg (www.blawg.com) and Legal Blog Watch (http://legalblogwatch.typepad.com), collect legal blogs of national interest. The Gallagher Law Library maintains a list of law-related blogs in Washington (http://lib.law.washington.edu/ref/blogswa.html).

XII. *Washington Legal Researcher's Deskbook 3d*

Washington Legal Researcher's Deskbook 3d (2002) (the "*Deskbook*"), published by the Gallagher Law Library at the University of Washington, is the most comprehensive and in-depth book on researching Washington law. The *Deskbook* provides detailed explanations of how to find specific primary and secondary sources and includes information on specific topics such as Indian Law, local government law, and historical and archival research. It is a valuable resource for practicing attorneys (and law students) who need to research a variety of different legal subjects. A new edition of the deskbook is expected soon. The Gallagher Law Library also maintains an "Internet Legal Resources" webpage that highlights Washington state legal resources. The webpage address is http://lib.law.washington.edu/research/research.html.

XIII. Citing Secondary Authority

Secondary sources provide an excellent way to learn about an unfamiliar area of law and to find primary legal materials such as cases and statutes. But the bulk of your legal analysis, whether in an internal memo or a document filed with a court, should focus on primary authority. Indeed, a lawyer or law clerk ordinarily would not cite certain secondary sources—for example, encyclopedias, ALR annotations, or practice guides—except to describe to a colleague or supervisor where he or she found information.

Other more authoritative secondary sources such as leading treatises or law review articles appear more frequently in both internal memos and documents filed in courts, at least for certain purposes. For example, if no case provides a summary of trends in the law, citing a treatise or law review article that traces that development can help your reader understand these trends. Citing secondary authority is also appropriate when you are writing about a new legal issue or when you are arguing to expand or change the law. In these situations, a secondary source such as a treatise or law review article may be your only support. Finally, in some instances, citing an article or treatise written by a respected expert on the topic can strengthen an argument supported by primary authority.

Whether or not you cite to a secondary source in your analysis, you must decide the weight to give secondary authority. When evaluating the weight of secondary authority, consider first how well reasoned the analysis in that source is. In addition, the following criteria can help you determine the value of the source:

Who is the author? The views of a respected scholar, acknowledged expert, or judge carry more weight than a student author or an anonymous editor.

When was the material published? Especially for cutting-edge issues, a more recent article is likely to be more helpful. Even with more traditional issues, be sure that the material analyzes the current state of the law.

Where was the material published? Articles published in established law journals are generally granted the most respect. How well established a law journal is depends on the length of the journal's existence and the prestige of the school publishing the journal. Thus, a journal that has been published for a century at a top law school will carry more respect than a journal at a new, unaccredited school. On the other hand, a publication specific to your jurisdiction or dedicated to a particular topic may be more helpful than a publication from another state or one with a general focus.

What depth is provided? The more focused and thorough the analysis, the more useful the material will be.

How relevant is the source to your argument? If the author is arguing your exact point, the material will be more persuasive than if the author's arguments are only tangential to yours.

Has this secondary source been cited previously by the courts? If a court has found an article persuasive in the past, it is likely to find it persuasive again.

If you do rely on a secondary source in your analysis, be sure to provide appropriate attribution. Norms of attribution may differ in some circumstances in legal writing, but while in an academic setting it is best to err on the side of documenting your sources thoroughly.

XIV. Conclusion

Secondary sources are plentiful; which secondary source you use depends on your research goals. For a broad overview, an encyclopedia may be best. For in-depth analysis on a narrow topic, a law review article is more likely to be helpful. On cutting-edge issues, CLE material often covers new areas of law quickly. In litigation, court-approved forms and pattern jury instructions will be indispensable.

Consider your own background in the subject matter and the goals of your research, and select from these sources accordingly. A source that was not helpful in your last research project may be perfect for the current project. How many secondary sources you use depends on the success of your early searches and the time available to you. It would not be prudent to check every source discussed in this chapter.

Chapter 4

Statutes, Constitutions, and Court Rules

Statutes can affect almost every legal issue you deal with in practice. Often a statute will define your client's rights or responsibilities. A statute may set penalties for failure to comply with its requirements. Some statutes address new issues that are not dealt with at common law (e.g., the use of electronic signatures). Other statutes may codify or alter the common law (e.g., making embezzlement a felony). Even when no statute affects the substance of a claim, a statute of limitations may limit the time period during which you may bring a claim. Because of the breadth of issues covered by statutes and because they can alter the common law, statutes are often the first primary authority to consult when analyzing a legal problem.

I. Researching Washington Statutes

In many cases, your initial research in secondary sources, such as *Washington Practice*, will lead you to the key statutes that govern the legal problem you are researching. If so, your initial statutory research will involve little more than retrieving and updating the statutes for which you already have citations. Sometimes, however, you will need to search for statutes without much guidance from secondary sources. Table 4.1 outlines a general research strategy for those kinds of searches.

The remainder of this section discusses the different ways in statutes are published, organized, and enhanced; and it discusses in more depth how to find statutes and related case law.

Table 4.1 Outline for Washington Statutory Research

1.	Generate a comprehensive list of research terms.
2.	If doing research in print, look up these research terms in the index to one of the statutory codes.
3.	If doing research online, use these research terms to run a terms and connectors search in an annotated code database or look through a table of contents to find references to relevant statutes.
4.	Locate, update, and read the statutes.
5.	Use the statutes' annotations to find citations to cases that interpret or apply the statutes.
6.	Update the annotations.
7.	Read and analyze the relevant cases.

A. Session Laws — *Laws of Washington*

The Washington legislature meets every year. Regular legislative sessions start in January and last for 105 days in odd-numbered years and 60 days in even-numbered years. The Governor may also call special legislative sessions to address specific issues. Each year, the laws passed by the legislature during a session, called *session laws*, are published in chronological order in the *Laws of Washington*. Each session law has a *chapter number*, indicating when it was passed during that session (e.g., the first session law would be Chapter 1).

B. Official Code — *Revised Code of Washington*

It would be very difficult to research a legal issue if the only version of the statutes you had was the *Laws of Washington*. You would need to know the exact law you were looking for and the session when the legislature passed the law. For this reason, the laws are *codified*, meaning grouped according to subject matter, into the *Revised Code of Washington* (RCW). The RCW is a compilation of the session laws arranged by topic, with amendments added and repealed laws removed. It is the official source for Washington statutory law.

Table 4.2 Examples of Chapters and Sections in Title 9A, Washington Criminal Code

9A.46	Harassment.	
9A.48	Arson, reckless burning, and malicious mischief.	
9A.49	Lasers.	← Chapters
9A.50	Interference with health care facilities or providers.	
9A.52	Burglary and trespass.	
	9A.52.010 Definitions.	
	9A.52.020 Burglary in the first degree.	
	9A.52.025 Residential burglary.	
	9A.52.030 Burglary in the second degree.	
	9A.52.040 Inference of intent.	← Sections
	9A.52.050 Other crime in committing burglary punishable.	
	9A.52.060 Making or having burglary tools.	
	9A.52.070 Criminal trespass in the first degree.	
	9A.52.080 Criminal trespass in the second degree.	

Source: *Revised Code of Washington* (2008).

The RCW and its index take up nine volumes (numbered 0 through 8). Every other year there is also a supplemental volume. The RCW is divided into ninety-one titles, each covering a particular subject. For example, Title 5 covers "Evidence"; Title 9A[1] covers the "Washington Criminal Code"; Title 26 covers "Domestic Relations." RCW titles are further subdivided into chapters, and the chapters are divided into sections. Table 4.2 shows some of the chapters in Title 9A, and some of the sections in Chapter 9A.52.

The citation for the second-degree burglary statute is RCW 9A.52.030. Notice that citations do not include the names of the titles, chapters, or sections but simply the abbreviation "RCW" and the statute number.

---

1. If a letter appears after the title number, it simply means that the title was added between two existing titles. This may occur when a large part of an existing title is recodified. For example, many of the chapters in Title 9 ("Crimes and Punishments") were repealed and re-enacted; the chapters now appear in Title 9A ("Washington Criminal Code").

Every state's statutes are codified in this general manner, though the names vary from state to state. Examples include *Oregon Revised Statutes*, *Alaska Statutes*, and *Consolidated Laws of New York*. Citation manuals list the name of the statutory code for each state; see Table 1 in *The Bluebook* or Appendix I in the *ALWD Citation Manual*.

The RCW includes the text of the statutes. In addition, after the text of each statutory section you will find a bracketed list of citations to the session laws that originally enacted and that amended the section. Chapter 9, which addresses legislative history, explains how to read these citations. Always check the session law dates to make sure that you are looking at the version of the statute that governs your client's situation. For example, if your client's cause of action arose before an amendment, you may need to find the previous version of the statute.

C. Unofficial Annotated Codes—*Revised Code of Washington Annotated* and *Annotated Revised Code of Washington*

In addition to the official code, there are two unofficial versions of Washington's code: the *Revised Code of Washington Annotated* (RCWA), published by West; and the *Annotated Revised Code of Washington* (ARCW), published by LexisNexis. Both codes use the same numbering system as the RCW. For example, RCW 9A.52.030 refers to the same statute as RCWA 9A.52.030 and ARCW 9A.52.030.

The main difference between the RCW and the two unofficial codes is that in the unofficial codes *annotations* follow the text of each statutory section. For this reason, the unofficial codes are often called *annotated codes*.

Annotations are editorial enhancements added by the publisher to help researchers understand and interpret the statute. The annotations contain (1) historical information, (2) cross-references to other relevant statutes, and (3) citations to primary and secondary authority. Both annotated codes include this information following the text of the statute, but the order in which the information appears varies between the codes.

The first type of information in an annotated code is historical information. In addition to session law references, the historical information in the annotated codes frequently includes the text of previous versions of the statute. This information can help you understand the origin of the statute and how it changed over time. It can also help you figure out whether cases interpreting the statute have been rendered obsolete by later amendments.

In addition to listing historical information, the annotated codes cross-reference related Washington code sections. These cross-references point to important context and can help you interpret your statute. But remember that other statutory sections may be relevant to your research even though they are not listed.

Both annotated codes include *Notes of Decisions* or *case squibs,* which are short, one-sentence summaries of cases and attorney general opinions that interpret or apply the statute in question. For statutes that have generated a large number of lawsuits, the publisher groups summaries under descriptive headings and includes a table of contents.

The annotated codes also include references to relevant articles and legal encyclopedia entries. When using these lists of secondary authority, keep in mind that the annotated code you are using will generally list only proprietary sources published by its affiliates. For example, although both codes include law review articles from the journals of all three Washington law schools, only the RCWA (a West product) includes references to *Washington Practice* (a legal encyclopedia published by West and described more fully in Chapter 3).

D. The Research Process

How you begin to research Washington statutes depends on the information you have when you begin. Sometimes, you may know which statutes control your client's situation. For example, a colleague or supervisor may suggest you research RCW 9A.52.030 because the police have arrested your client for burglary. In that case, you can look up the statute either in a print version of the code or online. In print, this involves locating the volume that contains the title and chapter of your statute and turning to the appropriate page. Online, click on either "Get a Document" (LexisNexis) or "Find by citation" (Westlaw) and type in the citation. You can also easily find the statute (but no annotations) for free on the MRSC legal research website or on the legislature's website.

Often, you will begin research without knowing the particular statute you need to research. In that situation, consult secondary sources, as described in Chapter 3, and try to find an authoritative source that points you to the statute or statutes you need to resolve your legal problem. If you cannot find a secondary source that gives you guidance, search for statutes in the codes themselves. To do that, follow the outline at the beginning of this chapter in Table 4.1, which is explained in more detail below.

1. Generate a List of Research Terms

To find all the statutes that may relate to your issue, develop an expansive list of research terms. Use the journalistic approach or the TARPP method from Chapter 2. Refer to Table 2.3 for an example of research terms in a burglary case.

2. Search the Index

To research in print, find your research terms in the index volumes for the RCW, the RCWA, or the ARCW, which are found at the end of the set. Be flexible and search for all the terms you brainstormed. As you find the terms in the index volumes, write down the statutory references. See Table 4.3 for examples from an entry in the RCWA index.

Do not stop reviewing the index after finding just one statutory reference; several statutes may address your issue. Note that the Latin abbreviation "et seq" refers to the statute listed and the sections that follow it. Sometimes a research term will be included in the index but will be followed by a cross-reference to another index term. Following these cross-references may lead you to relevant statutes.

Table 4.3 Selected Entries for BURGLARY in RCWA Index

Generally, 9A.52.010 *et seq.*
Capital punishment, aggravating circumstances, 10.95.020
Definitions, 9A.52.010
Domestic Violence, 10.99.010 *et seq.*
First degree burglary, 9A.52.020
Juvenile delinquents and dependents, jurisdiction, 13.04.030
Residential burglary, 9.94A.515, 9A.52.025
Second degree burglary, 9A.52.030

Source: *West's Revised Code of Washington Annotated*, General Index, A to L (2008). Reprinted with permission of West, a Thomson Reuters business.

To research online, look for your research terms in an online index just as you would in a print index. Currently, only Westlaw offers an online index to the code. This database, "Washington Statutes—General Index" (WA-ST-IDX), is listed on the Washington research tab. Select this database and then run a terms and connectors search in the index. Because you are searching for entries in an index, you probably should not use the connector "and" unless you think the index entry will contain both terms.

Keep in mind that you are searching the full text of the index. Westlaw will look for your terms anywhere in the index, not just where one appears as an individual entry or subentry. For example, if "burglary" is your search term, you will get a list of every entry under which the word "burglary" appears, not just the main entry for "burglary." To retrieve only main entries, search using the "citation" field, CI( ), and put your search term inside the parentheses.

Another way to find statutes online using your research terms is to run a terms and connectors search in the full text of the statutes. From the Washington research page, you can search the full text of the ARCW on LexisNexis and the RCWA on Westlaw (WA-ST-ANN). If you use these databases, you will be searching in the annotated code, which means your search will include not just the text of the statute, but also the annotations. In some cases, this can be a drawback because you will retrieve a large number of irrelevant results. To exclude the annotations, search an unannotated version of the code on Westlaw, using the database WA-ST. LexisNexis does not provide access to an unannotated version of the code but does permit you to exclude annotations from your results. For example, to search for statutory provisions that focus on drinking water, but not case annotations on this topic, use a segment restriction, either unannotated: "unanno(drinking w/5 water)," or text: "text(drinking w/5 water)."

Finally, you can scan a code's table of contents for relevant sections. Remember from Chapter 2 that a table of contents online is usually expandable, meaning you can click on an entry and see subentries. When looking at an online table of contents for the Washington code, you will first see just the names of the titles. By clicking on the "+" sign next to a title name, the title entry will expand, and you will see a list of all of the chapters under the title. By clicking on the "+" sign next to the chapter name, you will see all of the sections under the chapter.

Table of contents searching is an especially effective way to find statutes online. You can use your search terms to help you figure out which entries to expand without inefficiently searching the full text of documents. For example, if you search for the burglary statute discussed above, you can review the list of titles and will probably realize that the burglary statute appears under either one of two titles, "Crimes and Punishments" or "Washington Criminal Code." As soon as you expand "Washington Criminal Code," you will see a chapter entitled "Burglary and Trespass" (if you expand "Crimes and Punishments," you will immediately see "repealed" next to the "Burglary" chapter and will know that the current burglary statute must be located somewhere else). If you expand the "Burglary and Trespass" chapter, you will see the names of all the burglary statutes in this chapter, including "9A.52.030 Burglary in the second degree." This method of searching also has the advantage of providing context by automatically showing you the names of the neighboring statutes. For example, you will see that the first section under the burglary chapter is "Definitions." Other search methods might not make the existence of that section as apparent.

To access a table of contents on LexisNexis, click on the name of the source you would like to search. If the source includes a table of contents it will be displayed below the search box. To access a table of contents on Westlaw, click on the database you would like to search and then click on the "Table of Contents" link that appears below the research page tabs.

When deciding how to search for statutes, keep in mind that searching the entire text of the code is usually not as reliable or productive as searching an index or table of contents. A full-text search generally produces too many results, many of which may not be relevant. Index and table of contents searches allow you to avoid hit or miss searching and gain the benefits of conceptual searching.

3. Find and Read the Statutory Language

For each statutory section that you find in the index, select the volume of RCW, RCWA or ARCW that contains the title of your statute, and then find the statute itself. If you are working online, you may want to print out the statute you are working with. Since you often have to flip around in the code to find definitions or cross-references, working with statutes online can be cumbersome. You will need to be ready to go back online to read related sections, and you may even want to switch over to the print versions of the code or use them in conjunction with the online versions.

Once you find a relevant statute, look at the nearby sections. Remember that the sections are grouped by subject; to understand a single statute you may have to read other, related statutes. One statute may contain general provisions while another contains exceptions to the general rule. Always look for a "Definitions" section. These sections define the terms used in subsequent sections.

When you read a statute, you should always also review the historical notes at its end. Chapter 9 explains in detail how to read the bracketed historical information, but, in general, look at the dates (which indicate when the legislature made changes to the statute) and compare them to the dates relevant to your client's case. As noted above, if your client's situation is governed by a previous version of the statute, you can use the information in the historical notes section to determine if the changes affect the outcome of your case. If

Figure 4.1 Example of a Washington Statute

9A.52.030. Burglary in the second degree

(1)   A person is guilty of burglary in the second degree if, with intent to commit a crime against a person or property therein, he enters or remains unlawfully in a building other than a vehicle or a dwelling.

(2)   Burglary in the second degree is a class B felony.

[1989 2nd ex.s. c 1 § 2; 1989 c 412 § 2; 1975—'76 2nd ex.s. c 38 § 7; 1975 1st ex.s. c 260 § 9A.52.030]

Source: RCW 9A.52.030.

you are using an annotated code, the historical notes that follow the bracketed information will usually describe what changes the legislature made to the statute.

Figure 4.1 sets out an example of a Washington statute. Note that like most other statutory sections, it is further divided into subsections.

After you find the statute you want, read it very carefully. Too many researchers fail to take the time necessary to read the language of the statute and consider all of its implications before deciding whether it is relevant to the research problem. And because few statutes are so clear that they can be understood in one reading, careful research generally requires you to read a statute several times before you understand its meaning and relevance.

To guarantee that you understand the statute, break it into elements—or basic requirements. If any element or requirement is missing, the statute does not apply. Using bullet points or an outline format is helpful for identifying each element. Connecting words and punctuation provide guidance for the relationships between different requirements of the statute. Small words like "and" and "or" can drastically change the meaning of a statute. The word "and" indicates a separate element that must be present for the statute to apply; the word "or" indicates an alternative element. Note, too, the difference between "shall," which requires action, and "may," which is permissive. In Table 4.4, RCW 9A.52.030 is broken into its three elements.

Table 4.4 Elements of RCW 9A.52.030 (Second-Degree Burglary)

1. With intent to commit a crime against
    a. a person therein or
    b. property therein
2. he
    a. enters or
    b. remains unlawfully
3. in a building other than a
    a. vehicle or
    b. dwelling

One caveat: Before you spend time reading a statute carefully, you will want to make sure it is the most recent version, or the version that applies to your client's situation. Updating is discussed below in its own section.

4. Find Relevant Cases Interpreting the Statutory Language

You will most often do your research using the annotated codes because they summarize cases interpreting the statutory language. Legislatures write statutes generally so that they apply to a wide array of circumstances. To be able to predict how a court may apply a statute in a particular case, you must know how the courts have interpreted and applied the statute in the past.

You need not read every case listed in the annotations. Review the case summaries strategically to see if the case is relevant to the issue you are researching. Table 4.5 summarizes factors to consider when deciding whether to read a case listed in the annotations.

Keep in mind that publishers group the cases under descriptive headings; use these headings to help you find cases that address the same issue as your case. In addition, note that cases are listed in reverse chronological order under each heading, so you will find the most recent cases listed first.

Table 4.5 Factors to Consider When Deciding
Which Cases to Read

1. **Mandatory over persuasive authority**

    The annotated statutes will include not just cases from state courts in Washington, but also cases from federal courts in Washington. Although a federal court may interpret or apply a Washington statute, the court's analysis of Washington law is not binding on Washington courts.

    Note that the opinions from one division of the Washington Court of Appeals are not necessarily binding authority on other divisions. Whenever possible, choose cases from the division that has jurisdiction in your case.

2. **Newer cases over older cases**

    Newer cases are usually written in more modern-day English and often summarize the current state of the law.

3. **Cases that are factually similar over those that are less similar**

    Some case summaries include facts of the case as well as points of law. Read cases that are *factually* similar to yours; however, do not confuse this with reading only cases that reach a *result* similar to the result your client would like. If a case is factually similar but reaches a result that would be bad for your client, you will need to find a way to distinguish the case or find an alternative legal basis for your claim.

4. **Cases with specific information over those with general information**

    As noted above, some case summaries will include facts as well as points of law. If the facts are similar to your client's facts, read these cases before resorting to cases that only have general summaries.

5. Update

Updating is crucial to accurate research; the law is in constant flux, and you need to make sure that you have the most recent information. Although updating is discussed here in its own section, with statutes you will want to update as you go, both after you find what appears to be a relevant statute and after you find relevant cases in the annotations. Updating as you go will ensure that you do not spend time reading and analyzing out-of-date material. This section discusses how to update statutes using both print and online sources. As you read this discussion, keep in mind that updating statutes using print sources is more cumbersome than it is using Westlaw or Lexis-Nexis. After you learn the updating process, you will probably want to use the online method or a combination of the two methods.

a. Updating Print Sources

The basic process for updating all print sources is the same; the main difference is in terminology. To update most print sources, you should look in the pocket part or supplement for more recent information once you have checked the main volume. With codes, the updating process is a bit more complex. After you find your statute in the main volume, check the pocket part or supplement. The *preface* to a pocket part or supplement will tell you the pocket part or supplement's cut-off date (for example, the preface may tell you the pocket part includes laws through the 2008 Regular Session). A preface is an introduction and is usually on the first or second page of a source. If the legislature has been in session since the cut-off date, you will need to check the session laws to see whether the legislature has enacted a change that has not yet been codified.

In Washington, you can check the session laws by using *West's Washington Legislative Service*, which is a set of paper booklets that publishes the session laws before they are available in the *Laws of Washington*. At the back of each booklet is a table of RCW sections affected by the session laws. See if your statute section is listed in the table. If it is, you will need to review that session law. The table in each booklet is *cumulative* (information from an earlier edition is incorporated into a newer edition) for the legislative session, so you only need to check the most recent booklet.

To find more recent cases interpreting your statute, first check the code's pocket part or supplement and then check the reporter's advance sheets. You can use the official advance sheets or those for the

Pacific Reporter. (Chapter 5 explains reporters and advance sheets in detail.) Review the subject index at the front of any advance sheet issued since the cut-off date of the code's pocket part or supplement to see if the advance sheet contains any cases relevant to your research.

b. Updating Online

Even though the information available on LexisNexis and Westlaw is more current than what is available in print, you still need to update any statutes that you find online. If the legislature is in session, or if the session laws have not yet been incorporated into the RCW, there could be changes to a statute that are not yet reflected in the online codes.

Fortunately, updating a statute online is much easier than it is in print. On LexisNexis, if there are any recent session laws that affect your statute, a bold "Status" line will appear before the text of the statute with links to those laws. This status line will not include any *pending* legislation that could affect your statute, only bills that have been *passed.* The top of the document will tell you the cut-off date for the annotations. To find more recent cases, you will need to (1) run a terms and connectors search using the statute number and a date restriction as the search terms, or (2) Shepardize the statute (a process described in Chapter 7).

On Westlaw, a red flag at the top of the page indicates that there are either (1) session laws that have amended, repealed, or superseded the statute or (2) cases that have found the statute invalid. If you click on the flag, you will see links to these laws or cases. A yellow flag at the top of the page indicates that there are either (1) session laws or pending bills that could affect the statute, or (2) cases that have limited the statute or called into question the validity of the statute (or a previous version of the statute). Clicking on the yellow flag will take you to a list of links to these bills or cases.[2] The annotations on West-

---

2. The "History" link in the left frame will also take you to the same information as the flags.

law are as current as the cases available on Westlaw, so you will not need to run a separate terms and connectors search.

You can also see if there are any session laws that have amended or repealed your statute by checking the legislature's website (www.leg.wa.gov/legislature). Current legislative information is available on this first page. Historical bill information is available at http://apps.leg.wa.gov/billinfo. On this page, you will find a table of RCW sections affected (as in the print version of *West's Washington Legislative Service*). You can also access the text of the session laws on this site.

6. Read the Cases that Your Research Reveals

Once you have decided which cases you want to read, retrieve them, either online or in the reporters. Prioritize the cases using the same factors as you did in first deciding which cases to read. For example, read cases that are mandatory authority before those that are persuasive; generally read newer cases before reading older ones.

As you start reading each case, first quickly skim the synopsis and headnotes (editorial features covered in Chapter 5) to see whether the case appears to be on point. Find the relevant headnotes and skim the corresponding parts of the case. Skim that portion of the case. Only after doing that should you consider photocopying, or printing, or taking extensive notes.

In addition to taking notes on individual cases, pay attention to how the cases fit together. Look for trends in the law and in the facts of the cases. Has the interpretation of the statute remained unchanged? Have certain facts virtually guaranteed success for one party while other facts have tended to cause difficulties?

Do not forget to compare the date the court decided the case with the date of any amendments to the statute noted in the historical notes. If the legislature has amended the statute since the date of the case, review the historical notes to make sure the amendments did not change the statute in a way that would have made a difference in the case.

E. When to Use the Official Code

The text of a statute often will not answer your legal question; you will need to use the annotations to find authorities that help you understand and apply the statutory language. For that reason, you will most often use the annotated codes to do your research. However, remember that the RCW is the official code and that you will need to cite the official code when quoting or otherwise referring to a statute. In addition, some attorneys use the official code when they want to flip quickly between sections or to see how neighboring sections relate to one another. Both tasks are easier to do in the official code (nine volumes) than in the RCWA (close to 100 volumes) or the ARCW (close to thirty volumes).[3]

II. Researching Other State Statutes

While the same basic process applies to statutory research in other states, some important differences deserve note. First, different states use different numbering systems. Some states, like Washington and Oregon, use only numbers to identify a statute (e.g., Wash. Rev. Code § 9A.52.030 and Or. Rev. Stat. § 164.215). California statutes, by contrast, include both a subject title and a section number. For example, the formalities of summons in a civil action are covered in Section 412.20 of the "Civil Procedure Code." The citation is Cal. Civ. Pro. Code § 412.20.

Also, not all states have two unofficial codes. For example, Oregon has only one unofficial code (published by West). Alaska does not have an unofficial code; its only code is the official code. Some offi-

---

3. RCWA volumes are smaller than ARCW volumes. But another reason the RCWA has more volumes than the ARCW is that the RCWA has more annotations. This does not mean, however, that the RCWA is necessarily a "better" resource. The RCWA editors seek to provide comprehensive coverage of citing references while the ARCW editors seek to provide selective, focused annotations. Although you find more cases listed in the RCWA annotations, many cases mention the statute only briefly.

cial codes, like Oregon's and Alaska's, contain annotations. Annotations in an official code may not be as complete or current as the annotations in an unofficial code, in which case you will need to do additional research in a digest (see Chapter 6) to find more cases interpreting the statutes. A reference librarian can give you more information about these kinds of jurisdictional variations.

III. Researching Federal Statutes

The official text of federal statutes is published in the *United States Code* (USC). Federal statutes are *codified* (arranged by subject) in the USC under fifty titles. Within each title, individual statutes are assigned section numbers. To cite a federal statute, you must include both the title and the section number. For example, the federal statute granting appellate jurisdiction to federal appellate courts is 28 USC § 1291 (2006); Title 28 is devoted to courts and judicial matters, and 1291 is the section number assigned to this statute. The date of publication of that volume is 2006.

The USC is reissued in a new edition every six years by the Government Printing Office (GPO) and updated between editions by annual bound supplements. Because the USC is updated infrequently and does not include annotations, it is of limited value to researchers.[4] The sources you are more likely to use are the *United States Code Annotated* (USCA) and *United States Code Service* (USCS).

Both the USCA and the USCS contain federal statutes and annotations to cases interpreting or applying the statutes. Some researchers prefer the USCA because it provides more case annotations than the USCS; others prefer the USCS because it provides a better index and more focused case annotations.

---

4. Note, however, that *The Bluebook* and the *ALWD Citation Manual* both require citation to the official code (the USC). If the current text is not yet available in the USC, you should cite to the USCA or the USCS. Citation is discussed in more detail in Appendix A.

The print versions of the USCA and the USCS are updated through pocket parts and paperback supplements. To be certain that you have the current statutory language, check the pocket parts at the back of each volume you use, as well as additional paperback supplements found at the end of each set. When only portions of the statute have changed, the pocket part may show the new language and refer to the unchanged language in the hardbound volume. Other pocket parts are cumulative, so a modified statute will be reprinted in full. Some researchers prefer to begin with the pocket part information, focusing on the most recent statutory language and annotations, and then refer back to the bound volume.

USCS is a LexisNexis publication, so you can find it only on Lexis-Nexis; USCA is a West publication, available only on Westlaw. If you are using the online codes, watch for the same updating indicators (e.g., a flag) as you would for state statutes.

IV. Constitutions

This chapter started with statutes rather than constitutions because, although constitutions are a higher authority, you will usually want to start your research with statutes. Moreover, Constitutions are published in statutory code sets, so searches for statutes retrieve constitutional provisions as well. Constitutions set out broad principles and are less likely to address your issue than statutes, which generally address more specific situations.

A. Researching the Washington Constitution

Researching the Washington Constitution is comparable to researching a Washington statute. Just as the RCW is divided into titles, the Washington Constitution is divided into *articles*, and each article is divided into sections.

You can find the text of the Washington Constitution in Volume 0 of the RCW. Annotated versions are available in both the ARCW and the RCWA and are available on LexisNexis and Westlaw. The indexes to the RCW, ARCW, and RCWA include references to relevant constitutional provisions. Consequently, if the Washington Constitution, rather than a Washington statute, governs the issue that you are researching, using the index will point you to the relevant constitutional provision. In addition, both Westlaw and LexisNexis allow you to search databases containing the text of both the constitution and the code.

B. Broader State Protections — the *Gunwall* Factors

One issue that arises in researching a state constitutional provision is whether the state constitution provides broader protection than the federal constitution. Although a state constitutional provision cannot take away rights granted by the federal constitution, a state constitutional provision can give more rights. For example, Article I, Section 7, of the Washington Constitution and the Fourth Amendment to the United States Constitution both restrict the government's ability to perform a search without a warrant. However, the Washington Supreme Court has said that the Washington Constitution provides greater protection of individual privacy than the United States Constitution. So, for example, although the United States Constitution does not require that the police obtain a warrant in order to search garbage left on the curb for collection, a warrantless search of curbside trash may violate the Washington Constitution.[5]

In determining whether the state constitution provides greater protection than the United States Constitution, Washington courts look at the following, non-exclusive, six factors: (1) the language of the state constitution (for example, the state provision may have no federal counterpart), (2) significant differences in the text of parallel provisions of the federal and state constitutions, (3) state constitutional and common law history, (4) pre-existing state law, (5) differences in structure between the federal and state constitutions, and (6) whether the provision addresses a matter of particular state interest or local concern (matters that are local in character may be more appropri-

---

5. *See State v. Boland*, 115 Wn.2d 571, 800 P.2d 1112 (1990).

ately addressed by the state constitution).[6] Because these factors were first articulated in a case called *State v. Gunwall*, they are commonly known as the "*Gunwall* factors."[7]

An in-depth discussion of these factors is beyond the scope of this book, but if you are researching a constitutional issue, you should investigate whether the court will (or has already) examined the *Gunwall* factors in relation to your particular circumstances.

C. The United States Constitution

The federal constitution is published along with the Washington Constitution in Volume 0 of the RCW. Annotated versions are available in print in the first few volumes of USCA and USCS, and online on LexisNexis and Westlaw. You can find unannotated versions on many websites, including the U.S. House of Representatives website at (www.house.gov).

V. Court Rules

This chapter includes information on court rules because, although court rules are not enacted into law like statutes, they are often published with statutes.

Court rules govern many of the procedural aspects of an action. For example, although a statute sets out the elements of second-degree burglary, a court rule sets out what information the indictment charging the defendant must contain. Although some court rules can seem like "technicalities," success in litigation may depend as much on compliance with these rules as it does on the merit of the claim.

---

6. *See State v. Gunwall*, 106 Wn.2d 54, 720 P.2d 808 (1986).
7. *See* Hugh D. Spitzer, *New Life for the "Criteria Tests" in State Constitutional Jurisprudence: "Gunwall is Dead—Long Live* Gunwall*!*, 34 Rutgers L.J. 1169 (2006).

Court rules are written in outline form like statutes, and they should be researched like statutes. In other words, you need to read the court rule carefully and, when necessary, find cases that interpret the rule. In addition, most sets of court rules have an index where you can look up your research terms, just as you would with statutes. However, early in your legal career, you may have difficulty knowing whether an issue will be governed by a court rule or by a statute. For that reason, unless you have been given the citation to a specific court rule or can use an index that includes court rules and statutes, you should first consult a secondary source (discussed in Chapter 3) to determine whether you should rely on the code or on the court rules.

A. Washington Court Rules

In Washington, there are both state and local court rules. The state rules, which are adopted by the Washington Supreme Court, include sets of rules that apply to all courts—the appellate courts, the superior courts, and the courts of limited jurisdiction. Some of these sets are further subdivided. For example, the rules for superior courts include civil and criminal rules.

Local court rules apply only to a particular superior, district, or municipal court. For example, Pierce County Superior Court has its own set of local rules. Local rules tend to address more specific matters than state rules. The rules are not mutually exclusive; for example, both the state and the local court rules govern practice in Pierce County Superior Court.

1. Using Print Sources for Court Rules

The court rules are printed in several places. You can find the text of the state and local rules in *Washington Court Rules: State* and *Washington Court Rules: Local Rules*. These are both soft-cover books, and they are republished every year. At the front of each set of state and local rules there is a "Table of Rules" much like a table of contents; there is also an index after each set of state rules (e.g., after the Rules for Superior Courts).

In addition, just as there are annotated versions of the RCW, there are annotated versions of the state court rules (the local rules are not annotated). The *Washington Rules of Court Annotated* is part of the ARCW (the code published by LexisNexis). This three-volume set consists of two volumes with annotated state rules and one volume with unannotated local rules. An index follows each set of rules, and the state rules are also indexed in the main ARCW index.

You can also find annotated court rules in *Washington Court Rules Annotated*. Although this is a West publication, it is not part of the RCWA. This three-volume set contains all the state rules, with an index after each set of rules. West also publishes *Washington Practice*, which is a legal encyclopedia discussed more fully in Chapter 3. *Washington Practice* includes a title called "Rules Practice" in which the text of each state court rule is set out, along with an explanation and citations to cases interpreting the rule.

As with any legal source, you need to update court rules. Because the Washington Supreme Court adopts state court rules, changes in the state rules are made through orders of the Court. These orders are published in the advance sheets for *Washington Reports, 2d Series*. To update a court rule, you should check the table of contents in any advance sheets issued since the publication of the court rule. Because the rules are republished every year, you will not have to check very many advance sheets. The table of contents will tell you if that set of advance sheets contains any orders amending the rules. To update local rules, contact the specific court and find out if there have been any changes.

2. Using Online Sources for Court Rules

You can access the court rules online either by doing a full-text terms and connectors search or by using the table of contents feature. Just as finding statutes by using a full-text search can be difficult, finding court rules using a full-text search can be difficult. Unless you have the citation to a particular court rule, the most effective way to find relevant rules will probably be to use the table of contents feature. This allows you to see neighboring court rules that may also be relevant.

LexisNexis and Westlaw both have databases containing the annotated state rules and the local rules. Note that on LexisNexis you cannot search any of the court rule databases using a table of contents. Westlaw has recently added the "KeyRules" option to state and federal jurisdictional tabs. "KeyRules Washington" (KEYRULES-WA) integrates local county practice rules with statewide court rules, forms, and practice guides to assist practitioners with filing court documents.

One of the best places to access the court rules online for free is the Washington Courts website (www.courts.wa.gov). The website contains state as well as local rules (or links to local rules). You can navigate through the rules in a table of contents manner or run a terms and connectors search, although the searching capabilities are not as advanced as those on LexisNexis or Westlaw.

Remember to update any court rule you find online. Even court rules on the Washington Courts website can be out of date by several months, so you will still need to check the advance sheets for orders amending state rules. The website indicates when the court rules were last updated, so you will know how many advance sheets you need to check. You could also check the section of the Washington Courts website that posts proposed rules published for comment. See www.courts.wa.gov/court_rules. On LexisNexis, you can update state court rules by accessing the "Federal and State Court Orders" database from the Washington research page. From there, scroll down to "Washington," choose the appropriate time period, and browse through the list of orders to see if your rule number appears. On Westlaw, you can update by searching the "Washington Court Orders" database using your rule number as a search term along with a date field restriction.

To update local rules, the Washington Courts website and LexisNexis advise you to contact the court directly. Westlaw's "Washington Court Orders" database (WA-RULESUPDATES) includes local court orders, so you can run a search like the one described above using your rule number and date restriction (although it is still a good idea to contact the court to verify you have the most recent rule version).

B. Federal Court Rules

Similar rules exist on the federal level. They are published in *Washington Court Rules: Federal*, as well as in USC, USCA, and USCS. Placement of the rules varies among the statutory publications. For example, in USC and USCA, the Federal Rules of Appellate Procedure are just after Title 28. In USCS, the rules are at the end of all fifty titles in separate volumes devoted to rules. Each court may also have its own "local rules" with specific practices required by that court. Check the annotated codes or the court's website to learn about local rules.

You can locate cases relevant to federal rules using the annotated codes or by using one of the federal digests (described in the next chapter).

Chapter 5

Judicial Opinions and Reporters

A *judicial opinion*, also called a *case*, is written by a court to explain and justify its decision in a particular dispute. Cases are published in roughly chronological order in books called *reporters*. Some reporters include cases decided by only a certain court, for example, the Washington Supreme Court. Other reporters include cases from courts within a specific geographic region, for example, the western United States. Still other reporters publish only those cases that deal with a certain topic, such as bankruptcy, media law, or rules of civil procedure. Reporters that publish cases from a particular court or geographic area are the ones most commonly used by general practitioners.

I. Where to Find Washington Cases

A. Washington Reporters

All cases decided by the Washington Supreme Court are published in *Washington Reports*, which is divided into two sets or *series*. The first set, *Washington Reports*, has 200 volumes and contains cases decided from 1889 (when Washington became a state) until 1939. The second set, *Washington Reports, 2d Series*, currently has more than 150 volumes and contains cases decided from 1939 until the present. The abbreviation for *Washington Reports* is "Wash."; the abbreviation for *Washington Reports, 2d Series*, is "Wn.2d."[1] Cases in these re-

---

1. As explained in Chapter 1, footnote 7, most citations used in this book follow the rules from the *Style Sheet* used by the Washington courts. The reporter abbreviations under these rules are sometimes different from the rules

porters are cited as follows: *Sheldon v. Fettig,* 129 Wn.2d 601 (1996). The citation indicates that you can find this case in volume 129 of *Washington Reports, 2d Series,* starting on page 601, and that the Washington Supreme Court decided the case in 1996.

Washington's intermediate appellate court opinions are published in a separate reporter called *Washington Appellate Reports,* which has only one series and is abbreviated as "Wn. App." Cases in *Washington Appellate Reports* are cited as follows: *Vukich v. Anderson,* 97 Wn. App. 684 (1999). This citation indicates that you can find this case in volume 97 of *Washington Appellate Reports,* starting on page 684, and that the Washington Court of Appeals decided the case in 1999.

Not all cases are published in the reporters. All Washington Supreme Court cases are published, but the Washington Court of Appeals issues both published and *unpublished opinions* (also known as *unreported opinions*). The panel that decides a case determines whether the opinion has sufficient precedential value to be published.[2] If the panel decides not to publish an opinion, the case name will be listed, without an opinion, at the end of the appropriate volume of *Washington Appellate Reports.* This list of unpublished opinions always starts on page 1001. Therefore, if you have a citation to a case reported in *Washington Appellate Reports,* and the citation indicates the first page of the decision is 1001 or higher, you know that the opinion is unpublished.

As explained elsewhere in this book, you can find unpublished opinions on the Washington Courts website, on several commercial websites (including LexisNexis and Westlaw), and on some free websites. However, these cases have no precedential value, and a court rule[3] prohibits citing unpublished opinions of the Washington Court of Appeals as an authority in any Washington court.[4]

---

in *The Bluebook,* the *ALWD Manual,* and the rules from other state courts. For example, *Washington Reports, 2d Series,* is abbreviated "Wash. 2d" under *The Bluebook* and *ALWD* rules and "Wn.2d" under the *Style Sheet.*

2. RCW 2.06.040; RAP 12.3(d).

3. Court rules govern the procedural aspects of cases (e.g., the page limit for a brief). Court rules are covered in Chapter 4.

4. GR 14.1, Washington's non-citation rule, however, permits a party to cite an unpublished opinion from another jurisdiction if citation to the opin-

Cases from state trial courts in Washington are not published; in fact, few states publish opinions at the trial court level. You can obtain unpublished trial court opinions directly from the court that decided the case.

B. Regional Reporters

Washington Reports and *Washington Appellate Reports* are the official reporters for Washington appellate cases. But these cases are also published in a commercially produced *regional reporter* called *Pacific Reporter*, which has three series: *Pacific Reporter* (with 300 volumes), *Pacific Reporter, Second Series* (with 999 volumes), and *Pacific Reporter, Third Series* (where more recent opinions are published). While the text of a court's opinion is the same in the official and unofficial reporters, the appearance, pagination, and editorial enhancements may be different. The abbreviations for *Pacific Reporter* are "P." (first series), "P.2d" (second series), and "P.3d" (third series).

Pacific Reporter is called a regional reporter because it reports opinions from courts of several states located in the same region of the country. *Pacific Reporter* publishes cases from the courts of fifteen states: Alaska, Arizona, California, Colorado, Hawaii, Idaho, Kansas, Montana, Nevada, New Mexico, Oklahoma, Oregon, Utah, Washington, and Wyoming.[5] *Pacific Reporter* includes cases from the intermediate and highest appellate courts of most of these states. Other regional reporters are *North Eastern Reporter, Atlantic Reporter, South*

---

ion would be allowed in that jurisdiction. Thus, a party may cite unpublished federal opinions decided after January 1, 2007, in briefs submitted to Washington courts. *See* GR 14.1(b); Fed. R. App. P. 32.1.

5. If a state does not publish its own reporter, the regional reporter may be the official reporter. For example, the official reporter of Alaska cases is *Pacific Reporter*. The publisher, West, also publishes an offprint of *Pacific Reporter* that contains only Alaska cases, the *Alaska Reporter*. The appearance, pagination, and editorial enhancements are exactly like those in *Pacific Reporter*, but the books contain only the pages with cases from Alaska courts. A similar offprint of *Pacific Reporter* exists for Washington, the *Washington Reporter*, that contains only the pages with cases from Washington courts.

Eastern Reporter, Southern Reporter, South Western Reporter, and *North Western Reporter.* All of these regional reporters are published by West (the company that owns Westlaw). West decides which states to group together in regional reporters, and these groupings have no legal impact. The Appendix at the end of this chapter lists all of West's regional reporters and the states that West groups within each one.

Because some courts or law firms traditionally had access to only one set of the reporters, citation rules often require you to include use *parallel citations* (i.e., citations to both the official and the regional reporter) when you refer to a case. Two examples of parallel citations follow:

> *Sheldon v. Fettig,* 129 Wn.2d 601, 919 P.2d 1209 (1996).

> *Vukich v. Anderson,* 97 Wn. App. 684, 985 P.2d 952 (1999).

These parallel citations allow a reader to find the case in either Washington's official reporters or in the *Pacific Reporter.*

C. Advance Sheets

The bound volumes of reporters can take months to be published. To make cases available sooner, publishers supply subscribers with *advance sheets.* These pamphlets can be published much more quickly than hardbound books. Advance sheets for *Washington Reports* and *Washington Appellate Reports* are published on alternate weeks (i.e., *Washington Reports* one week and *Washington Appellate Reports* the next). The advance sheets for *Washington Reports* are yellow; advance sheets for *Washington Appellate Reports* are green. Libraries keep the advance sheets in binders, which are kept on the shelf near the reporters.

The pagination used in the advance sheets is the same as will be used in the hardbound volumes. Consequently, a citation to a case in the advance sheets will still be accurate after the case is published in the hardbound volumes. Although some lawyers still read the advance sheets because of the extra editorial content they provide, most lawyers now rely on the online slip opinions, which are available on the court's website.

D. Slip Opinions

To provide access to cases even faster than advance sheets, *slip opinions* are available from the court that decided the case and are typically released on the court's website on the date of the decision. A slip opinion is the official document produced by the court and sent to the parties. It does not contain editorial enhancements such as headnotes. For this reason, the slip opinion looks very different from the printed version in a reporter and requires a different citation form. If you need to cite a slip opinion, see a citation guide.

II. Anatomy of a Reported Case

A case printed in a reporter contains the exact language of the court's opinion. The reporter's publisher then adds supplemental information to help legal professionals read and understand the case, locate quickly the relevant parts of the case, and find related cases. The following discussion explains the information and enhancements included in recent volumes of *Washington Reports*. Most reporters will include the majority of these items, though perhaps in a different order. To best understand the following discussion, select a volume of *Washington Reports* from the library shelves or refer to the case excerpt in Figure 5.1 for examples of the concepts explained below. Note that this excerpt is from the official reporter, *Washington Reports*, so editorial enhancements are different from those in *Pacific Reporter*.

Docket Number. The number assigned to the case by a court is a docket number. Each court (i.e., trial court, Court of Appeals, or Supreme Court) will assign a different docket number to the case. Docket numbers are helpful in locating the parties' briefs, a court's orders, or other documents related to that case. Because most of these documents are not published, you can often obtain them only from the court that decided the case, and you usually must refer to the case by its docket number.

Notice that this section of the case also tells you that the case was decided *en banc* (see Chapter 1). In Court of Appeals opinions, this section will list the division that heard the case.

Figure 5.1 Case Excerpt

Sheldon v. Fettig, 129 Wn.2d 601 (1996)

[No. 63082-8. En Banc.]	Docket Number
Argued March 28, 1996. Decided August 1, 1996	Dates
PAMELA SHELDON, *Respondent* v. FRANCINE FETTIG, ET AL., *Petitioners*.	Parties and Procedural Designations
[1] Process—Service—Substitute Service—Statutory Provision Construction—Liberal or Strict Construction. RCW 4.28.080(15), which provides that substitute service of process may be effected by leaving a copy of the summons at the defendant's house of usual abode with a person of suitable age and discretion then resident therein, is liberally construed in order to effectuate service and uphold the jurisdiction of the court.	Headnote
[2] Process—Service—Substitute Service—Statutory Provision—Purpose. The purpose of RCW 4.28.080(15), which provides that substitute service of process may be effected by leaving a copy of the summons at the defendant's house of usual abode with a person of suitable age and discretion then resident therein, is to provide a reasonable means to serve defendants in a fashion reasonably calculated to accomplish notice.	Headnote
TALMADGE, J., DURHAM, C.J., and MADSEN, J., dissent by separate opinion; ALEXANDER, J., did not participate in the disposition of this case.	Procedural Information
Nature of Action: Action for damages resulting from an automobile accident. **Superior Court:** The Superior Court for Grant County, No. 92-2-00480-8, Kenneth L. Jorgensen, J., on September 15, 1993, denied the defendant's motion for a summary judgment and struck the defense of improper service of process, holding that service at the defendant's parents' home where a copy of the summons and complaint was left with the defendant's brother satisfied substitute service of process requirements. **Court of Appeals:** The court *affirmed* the decision of the trial court, holding that the plaintiff had effected valid substitute service of process. **Supreme Court:** Holding that the defendant's parent's house constituted a center of the defendant's domestic activity where she would most likely receive notice of the pendency of a suit if left with a family member, the court *affirms* the Court of Appeals and remands the case to the trial court for further proceedings.	Synopsis

Figure 5.1 Case Excerpt, *continued*

Sheldon v. Fettig, 129 Wn.2d 601 (1996)

Reed McClure, by *William R. Hickman;* and *Talbott, Simpson, Gibson, Davis &Bruns, P.S.,* by *Scott A. Bruns,* for petitioners. *Morris & Church,* by *Frank E. Morris* and *Shirley L. Bluhm,* for respondent.	Attorneys
TOTAL CLIENT-SERVICE LIBRARY® REFERENCES Am Jur 2d, Process §§ 198–226. ALR Index, Process and Service of Process and Papers	Library References
SANDERS, J.—The question in this case is the sufficiency of service of process where plaintiff attempted service of process by leaving a copy …	Start of Opinion

Source: *Washington Reports, 2d Series.* Reprinted with permission of West, a Thomson Reuters business. Note that some headnotes have been omitted for brevity and that the format has been modified slightly.

Dates. The reporter then lists the date the attorneys argued the case to the court and the date the court decided the case. Some reporters list just the date the court decided the case. For purposes citation, only the year the court decided the case is important.

Parties and Procedural Designations. All of the parties are listed with their procedural designations (e.g., "plaintiff"). The appealing party is called either the *appellant* or the *petitioner* depending on whether the appeal is taken as a matter of right or is discretionary. In either case, the opposing party is called the *respondent.*[6]

Headnotes. A headnote is a sentence or short paragraph that sets out a single point of law from a case. Most cases will have several headnotes. The text of each headnote often comes directly from the text of the opinion, but headnotes are generally not written by the court. For that reason, you should never rely on headnotes uncritically or cite them in legal documents. At the beginning of each head-

---

6. In Washington, the order of the parties' names remains the same throughout the litigation. In some jurisdictions, the parties' names can reverse at the appellate level depending on who files the appeal.

note is a number identifying it in sequence with other headnotes. Within the text of the opinion, the same number will appear next to the text supporting the headnote. Online, you can click on these headnote numbers to navigate through the case.

In *Washington Reports*, each headnote begins with several words or phrases in bold print. These words and phrases help you immediately see the area of law addressed by the headnote, and you can use them in subject indexes to locate other cases that discuss similar points of law. Unofficial reporters published by West also include terms (called "topics") following the headnote number. You can use these topics in digests to locate other relevant cases. (Subject indexes and digests are covered in Chapter 6.) Headnotes appear in both the official and regional reporters and on Westlaw and LexisNexis and differ slightly among the different sources.

Procedural Information. Procedural information includes the names of the judges who wrote opinions in the case and of any judge on the panel who did not participate in the decision. Note that following each name will be "J." for judge or justice or "C.J." for chief judge or justice.

Synopsis. One of the most helpful research aids included by the publishers is a synopsis. This is a short summary of the key facts, procedural history, legal points, and *disposition* of the case. The disposition of the case is the court's decision to affirm, reverse, remand, or vacate the decision below. If the appellate court agrees with only part of the lower court's decision, the appellate court may affirm in part and reverse in part. Reading a synopsis gives you a quick idea of whether a case is on point. But do not rely exclusively on a synopsis; at least skim the case headnotes to determine whether the case is important for your research. Synopses, like headnotes, are written by editors, not by the court. Never cite a synopsis, even when it gives an excellent summary of the case, because it is not authoritative.[7] Note that for Washington cases, LexisNexis includes a "case summary"

---

7. A *syllabus* is a case summary. For example, the Reporter of Decisions of the U.S. Supreme Court, in the course of publishing the Court's opinions, adds a *syllabus* to each case. Since the *syllabus* is not drafted by the Justices, it is not authoritative.

(with procedural posture, overview, and outcome) and LexisNexis headnotes; these appear before the court's official syllabus and headnotes.

Attorneys. Reporters provide the name of the attorney who represented each party and the law firm where the attorney worked. In addition, this section will also list the parties who submitted *amicus curiae briefs* in the case. An amicus curiae (Latin for "friend of the court") brief is filed by someone who is not a party to a case but who has a strong interest in the case.

Library References. Some reporters, including *Washington Reports*, cross-reference secondary sources, which can help you understand your legal issue or find additional authority. Like headnotes, library references are publisher-specific. Reporters cross-reference different publications, depending on their affiliations.

Opinion. In *Washington Reports*, the opinion begins with the name of the judge or justice who wrote the majority opinion. Judges or justices who disagree on the reasoning or outcome draft *concurring* or *dissenting* opinions. These appear at the end of the majority opinion. Though not binding, these opinions provide valuable insights and may be cited as persuasive authority. If there is no majority on both the reasoning and the outcome, the case will be decided by the opinion that garners the most support, or the *plurality decision*.

Parallel Citations. Publishers often provide citations to other reporters in which cases appear. *Washington Reports* includes parallel citations to the *Pacific Reporter* at the top of each page of the opinion (the parallel citation is not visible in the case excerpt in Figure 5.1).

At the back of each volume of *Washington Reports* (usually starting at page 1001), there is a list of petitions for review decided by the Washington Supreme Court. The Supreme Court rarely issues opinions when it grants, denies, or dismisses these petitions. Denying a petition does not mean that the Court agrees with the outcome or analysis in a lower court's opinion. Indeed, the fact that the court denied review in a particular case carries no precedential weight.

At the end of each volume of *Washington Reports* and *Washington Appellate Reports* is a subject index for the cases included in that volume. This index is an alphabetical list of the topics covered by the cases' headnotes, along with the first page of the case in which the headnote appears. West publishes a *Cumulative Subject Index* that collects the entries that appeared in the subject indexes of *Washington Reports* and *Washington Appellate Reports* from 1987 to date. This two-volume set is distributed to subscribers of the *Washington Reports* advance sheets. The *Cumulative Subject Index* can provide a quick way in print to identify recent cases by subject. Most researchers, however, will find the *Washington Digest* (discussed in Chapter 6) to be a more effective case-finding tool.

III. Access to Washington Cases Online

You can use either official or regional reporter citations to retrieve cases online. The main online providers covered in this section are LexisNexis, Westlaw, and the Municipal Research & Services Center (MRSC) legal research website. All three cover Washington case law starting with cases decided in 1854, the year the Washington Territory was created out of the Oregon Territory. When using other websites, always make sure you know the time period for which cases are available.

A. Commercial Providers

When you have a citation to a case, retrieving the document is as simple as typing the citation into the appropriate search box. To retrieve a case on LexisNexis, click on "Get a Document" and type in the citation. On Westlaw, click on "Find this document by citation" and type in the citation. When you access a case on Westlaw, you will notice that the screen is divided into two frames. The right frame contains the text of the case itself, and the left frame contains links to update the case. (Updating cases is discussed in Chapter 7.)

You can also find cases using the names of the parties or the docket number. On LexisNexis, after clicking on "Get a Document," simply click the tab for the "party name" or "docket number." On Westlaw, after clicking on "Find & Print," click on the link for "Find a Case by

Party Name." To find a case by the docket number on Westlaw, run a terms and connectors search in the Washington State Cases database using the field restriction for docket number, DN( ). The docket number goes inside the parentheses.

Cases are generally available on both services within a day after they are decided. Unlike the hardbound reporters, LexisNexis and Westlaw provide access to the full text of many unpublished court opinions (e.g., unpublished opinions from the Washington Court of Appeals).

LexisNexis and Westlaw show where the online text appears in the print reporters by inserting those page numbers into the online text at the print reporters' page breaks. This system is called *star pagination* because it identifies the different reporters by assigning each reporter either one or two asterisks. As you read a case, you will see one or two asterisks followed by a page number scattered throughout the text. The text that appears after the page number is located on that page in the print reporter. Star pagination allows you to provide *pinpoint* cites to particular pages in the print reporters, which is required by legal citation rules, even if you have read a case only online. Citation rules are covered in Appendix A.

B. Government and Organization Websites

As noted previously, you can access recent slip opinions on the Washington Courts website (www.courts.wa.gov/opinions). Opinions are available for ninety days after they are filed.

Washington case law (from 1854 to present) is available free on the Municipal Research & Services Center (MRSC) legal research website (www.legalWA.org). This site includes unpublished Washington Court of Appeals opinions, but only those filed since July 2007. Unfortunately, the MRSC website does not currently allow you to simply enter a citation to retrieve a case. Instead you will need to (1) search for the docket number, or (2) change the default search setting to "Search case titles only" and run a terms and connectors search using the parties' names connected by "and."

Note that the "About Our Data" section at the bottom of the MRSC search screen explains that MRSC draws on various sources —the official reporters, advance sheets, and slip opinions—for its data. Consequently, although the opinions on MRSC are generally available, you will need to double check the language and page numbers against the official reporters before filing a document with the court.

IV. Reporters for Federal Cases

So far this chapter has dealt with locating cases from Washington. The process for finding cases decided by federal courts is similar in many respects. Table 5.1 lists the federal court reporters, along with their citation abbreviations.

Table 5.1 Reporters for Federal Court Cases

Court	Reporter Name	Abbreviation
U.S. Supreme Court	*United States Reports* (official) *Supreme Court Reporter* *United States Supreme Court Reporter, Lawyers' Edition*	U.S. S. Ct. L. Ed. *or* L. Ed. 2d
U.S. Courts of Appeals	*Federal Reporter*	F. *or* F.2d *or* F.3d
U.S. District Courts	*Federal Supplement*	F. Supp. *or* F. Supp. 2d

A. United States Supreme Court

Decisions of the United States Supreme Court are reported in *United States Reports*, which is the official reporter; *Supreme Court Reporter*, which is a West publication; and *United States Supreme Court Reports, Lawyers' Edition*, another unofficial reporter. Although *United States Reports* is the official reporter, meaning that you should cite it if possible, that series frequently publishes cases several years after they are decided. Even the advance sheets can run several years late. Thus, for recent cases, you will often cite the *Supreme Court Reporter*. Another source for finding recent cases from the Supreme Court is *United States Law Week*. This service publishes the full text of cases from the Supreme Court and provides summaries of important decisions from state and federal courts.

There are a number of online sources for Supreme Court opinions. You can find opinions on LexisNexis and Westlaw, and the Court's own website (www.supremecourtus.gov) includes slip opinions soon after the decisions are rendered. An educational site supported by Cornell University (supct.law.cornell.edu/supct) also publishes opinions quickly.

B. United States Courts of Appeals

Selected cases decided by the federal intermediate appellate courts are published in *Federal Reporter*, a West publication now in its third series. The abbreviations for these reporters are F., F.2d, and F.3d. Some court of appeals cases that are not selected for publication in *Federal Reporter* are published in West's relatively new reporter series, *Federal Appendix*.[8]

You can find both published and unpublished courts of appeals opinions on LexisNexis and Westlaw. Limited access to recent opinions is also available on the U.S. Courts website (www.uscourts.gov) and the Cornell website (www.law.cornell.edu/federal/opinions.html).

C. United States District Courts

Selected cases from the United States District Courts, the federal trial courts, are reported in *Federal Supplement*, a West publication now in its second series. The abbreviations for these reporters are F. Supp. and F. Supp. 2d.

---

8. Before you cite a decision labeled "unpublished," you should consult relevant court rules on this point.

LexisNexis and Westlaw provide online access to district court opinions; some opinions are available on the U.S. Courts and Cornell websites listed above as well.[9]

V. Topical Reporters

Some reporters publish cases on a particular topic, rather than cases from a specific court or region. For example, *Federal Rules Decisions* includes federal trial court cases that analyze federal rules of civil and criminal procedure. Similarly, *Bankruptcy Reporter* includes cases from federal courts on that topic. Because these reporters are published by West, they contain West's editorial enhancements. Other publishers also provide reporters in topical areas. An example is *Media Law Reporter*, published by the Bureau of National Affairs, Inc. *Media Law Reporter* contains all relevant opinions of the United States Supreme Court, as well as significant opinions from federal and state courts, on the topic of media law.

VI. Reading and Analyzing Cases[10]

Once you locate a case, you must read it, understand it, and analyze its potential relevance to the problem you are researching. An attorney, judge, or client who has asked you to do the research will not be satisfied if you return from the library with a stack of printouts of cases you have not yet analyzed.

Do not expect reading a case to be easy. Understanding a case may take more mental work than you have ever dedicated to a few pages. It is not unusual for beginning lawyers to read complex cases at a rate of around fifteen pages per hour. Often this reading is interrupted by

---

9. Note that many federal district court cases involve jury trials. Written opinions are generally only available for cases decided by judges ("bench trials").

10. Part VI is based on materials drafted by Suzanne E. Rowe, editor, Carolina Academic Press Legal Research Series.

referring to a law dictionary to try to understand the terms used. Early efforts will be more productive if you have a basic understanding of civil procedure terms and the fundamental aspects of case analysis, and if you follow the strategies for reading cases outlined at the end of this chapter.

A. Key Terms

The person who believes he was harmed begins civil litigation by filing a *complaint* in the court he selects. The *plaintiff* is the person who files the complaint; the person against whom the complaint is filed is the *defendant*. The complaint names the parties, states the facts, notes the relevant laws, and asks for relief. Courts vary considerably in how much information is required at this stage of the litigation. In general, the complaint must be specific enough to put the defendant on notice of the legal concerns at issue and to allow him or her to prepare a defense. In Washington, only certain claims, such as fraud, must be stated with particularity.

The defendant has a limited amount of time in which to respond to this complaint. If the defendant does nothing within the prescribed time, the plaintiff can ask the court for a *default judgment*, which would grant the plaintiff the relief sought in the complaint. One form of response to the complaint is an *answer*. In the answer, the defendant admits to the parts of the complaint that he or she knows are true, denies those things that he or she disputes, and asserts no knowledge of other allegations. The defendant also may raise *affirmative defenses* in the answer. An affirmative defense is an assertion that would defeat the plaintiff's claim, even if all of the allegations in the complaint are true (e.g., self-defense).[11]

Throughout the litigation, parties submit a variety of papers to the court for its consideration. Some submissions, for example filing of a complaint, require no action or response from the court. Others ask the court to make a decision or take action. For example, a summary judgment motion asks the court to decide the case without having a trial.

---

11. *Black's Law Dictionary* 356 (Abridged 8th ed. 2005).

At trial, the parties may make motions that can be appealed. For example, during the trial, the plaintiff presents his evidence first. After all of the plaintiff's witnesses have testified, the defendant may move for *judgment as matter of law*, arguing that the plaintiff cannot win based on the evidence presented and asking for an immediate decision. An order granting that motion can be appealed.

Generally, appeals assert that the trial court made some kind of legal mistake that affected the outcome of the case and ask the appellate court to reverse the trial court's decision on that basis. If the appellate court agrees with the decision of the trial judge, it will *affirm*. If not, the court will *reverse* and, in some instances, *remand* the case back to the trial court for further proceedings.

Understanding the procedural posture of a case is crucial to understanding the court's holding. LexisNexis case summaries provide the case's procedural posture, preview the court's holding, and describe the procedural disposition of the case. These summaries, together with relevant rules of civil procedure, will help guide your analysis.

B. Fundamentals of Legal Analysis

Early in your career it may be difficult to determine whether a case is relevant to your research problem. If the case concerns the same *legally significant facts* as your client's situation, and the court applies law on point for your problem, then the case is relevant. Legally significant facts are those facts that affect the court's decision. Some attorneys call these outcome-determinative facts or key facts. Which facts are legally significant depends on the case. The height of the defendant in a contract dispute is unlikely to be legally significant, but that fact may be critical in a criminal case in which the only eyewitness testified that the thief was about five feet tall.

Your research will rarely reveal a case with facts that are exactly the same as your client's situation. Rather, several cases may involve facts that are similar to your client's situation but not exactly the same. Your job is to determine whether the facts are similar enough for a court to apply the law in the same way and reach the same outcome. If the court reached a decision favorable to your client, you will need to highlight the similarities. If the court reached an unfavorable decision from your client's perspective, you may argue that the case is distinguishable from yours based on its facts or that its reasoning is faulty. Keep in mind that you have an ethical duty to ensure that the court knows about a case from your jurisdiction directly on point, even if that case harms your client's legal position.

You are also unlikely to find one case that addresses all aspects of your client's situation. Clients can have several legal claims, and claims can themselves have several *elements* or *factors*. If a court decides that one element is not met, it might not discuss the others. In a different case, the court might decide that two factors are so overwhelming that others have no impact on the outcome. In these circumstances, you would have to find other cases that analyze the elements or factors that pertain to your client's case.

Once you determine that a case is relevant to some portion of your analysis, you must decide how heavily it will weigh in your analysis. Two important points need to be considered here. One is the concept of *stare decisis*; the other is the difference between *holding* and *dictum*.

Stare decisis means to "stand by things decided,"[12] and refers to the court's policy of following previous decisions. *Stare decisis* promotes consistency in the application of law and leads to more efficient decision making. Stare decisis may be either vertical or horizontal. *Vertical stare decisis* refers to the requirement that lower courts follow the decisions of higher courts. This requirement is limited, however, to courts within one jurisdiction. The Washington Court of Appeals must follow the decisions of the Washington Supreme Court, but not the decisions of courts of any other state.

The concept of *stare decisis* also requires courts to follow their own decisions in most cases. This is known as *horizontal stare decisis*. For example, the Washington Supreme Court should generally follow its own earlier cases in deciding new matters. Courts sometimes decide

---

12. *Black's Law Dictionary* 1173 (Abridged 8th ed. 2005).

not to follow a previous opinion, often because societal changes have chipped away at the previous opinion's reasoning or because the legislature has changed the legal landscape by enacting new statutes.

An interesting question relating to stare decisis sometimes arises in Washington: Do the three divisions of the Washington Court of Appeals have to follow each others' decisions? The answer is not entirely clear, but arguably a decision from one division is not binding on the other divisions.[13] In practice, the divisions do defer to each other most of the time. Still, when you research, try to rely on cases from the same division as your client's case when possible.

As noted, *stare decisis* requires courts to follow the prior cases' holdings. The *holding* is the court's decision on the legal issues raised by the case's facts. Other statements or observations that are not necessary to that decision are not binding; they are referred to as dicta. For example, a court in a property dispute may hold that the land belongs to X. In reaching that decision, the court may note that had the facts been slightly different, it would have decided the land belonged to Y. That observation does not address a legal issue raised by the case's facts and so is not binding on future courts. It may, however, be cited as persuasive authority and may carry some weight if it is well reasoned.

After finding a number of cases that have similar facts, discuss the same legal issue, and are binding, the next step is to synthesize the cases to state and explain the legal rule. Sometimes a court states the rule fully; if not, you will need to piece together the information from the relevant cases to state the rule completely, but concisely. Then use the analysis and facts of various cases to explain the law. Decide how the rule applies to your client's facts and determine

---

13. *See* Kelly Kunsch, *Stare Decisis: Everything You Never Realized You Need to Know*, Wash. St. Bar News, Oct. 1998, at 31. For example, in *Marley v. Department of Labor and Industries*, 72 Wn. App. 326, 330, 864 P.2d 960 (1993), Division One of the Court of Appeals expressly stated it was not bound and would not follow a Division Three opinion. The Washington Supreme Court then heard the case in order to resolve the conflict between the divisions. *Marley v. Dep't of Labor and Indus.*, 125 Wn.2d 533, 537, 886 P.2d 189 (1994).

your conclusion. Note that this method of synthesis involves much more than providing mere summaries of all the various cases. It involves a careful analysis of individual case holdings and what they mean when read together.

C. Reading Strategies

As you begin reading cases, the following strategies may help you understand them more quickly and more thoroughly.

- Review the synopsis to determine whether the case seems to be on point. If so, skim the headnotes to find the part of the case that is relevant. Remember that one case may discuss several legal issues, only one or two of which may interest you. Go to the part of the case identified by the relevant headnote and decide whether it pertains to your project.
- If the case is relevant, skim the entire case to get a sense of what happened and why, focusing on the part of the case identified by the relevant headnote.
- Read the case slowly and carefully. Skip parts that do not pertain to your problem. For example, if you are researching a property question, there is no need to scrutinize a tort issue arising in the same case. In modern opinions, issues are often set out in separate sections.
- At the end of each paragraph or page, consider what you have read. If you cannot summarize it, try reading the material again.
- Skimming text online or highlighting a printed page is often not sufficient to achieve a thorough comprehension of judicial opinions. The next time you read the case, read actively and take notes. The notes may be in the form of a "case chart" or scribbles that only you can understand. Regardless of the form of notetaking you use, the process of taking notes will help you identify and comprehend the case. Keep in mind that reading a case to prepare for class and reading a case to advise a client or prepare a legal document are two different tasks. Class notes and research notes may look different. Chapter 10 discusses taking notes on cases in more detail.

Appendix: Table of Reporter Coverage

Note that all of the reporters listed below are in at least their second series. For example, the *North Western Reporter* has a first and a second series, abbreviated "N.W." and "N.W.2d," respectively.

Regional Reporters and States Covered

Atlantic Reporter (A., A.2d)	Connecticut, Delaware, District of Columbia, Maine, Maryland, New Hampshire, New Jersey, Pennsylvania, Rhode Island, and Vermont
California Reporter (Cal. Rptr., Cal. Rptr. 2d)	California (covers Appellate Departments of the Superior Court in addition to the California Supreme Court and Court of Appeal.)
New York Supplement (N.Y.S., N.Y.S.2d)	New York (covers the N.Y. Supreme Court, Appellate Division and other lower courts in addition to the N.Y. Court of Appeals.)
North Eastern Reporter (N.E., N.E.2d)	Illinois, Indiana, Massachusetts, New York, and Ohio
North Western Reporter (N.W., N.W.2d)	Iowa, Michigan, Minnesota, Nebraska, North Dakota, South Dakota, and Wisconsin
Pacific Reporter (P., P.2d, P.3d)	Alaska, Arizona, California, Colorado, Hawaii, Idaho, Kansas, Montana, Nevada, New Mexico, Oklahoma, Oregon, Utah, Washington, and Wyoming
South Eastern Reporter (S.E., S.E.2d)	Georgia, North Carolina, South Carolina, Virginia, and West Virginia
South Western Reporter (S.W., S.W.2d, S.W.3d)	Arkansas, Kentucky, Missouri, Tennessee, and Texas
Southern Reporter (So., So. 2d), So. 3d	Alabama, Florida, Louisiana, and Mississippi

Chapter 6

Digests and Other Case Finding Tools

The previous chapter discussed judicial opinions and reporters but did not discuss strategies for finding cases. As with statutes, one of the best ways to locate cases is to rely on research already performed by experts (Chapter 3 discusses secondary sources). Digests and online digest equivalents allow you to supplement what you learn from secondary sources, and to find cases based on their subject in the absence of guidance from a secondary source.

The last chapter discussed how case reporters are organized chronologically. This structure makes it easy to find cases when you already have a citation. But reporters do not allow researchers to find cases based on their subject. Digests and their online equivalents fill this gap by classifying case law according to its subjects and allowing researchers to find very efficiently all the cases addressing a particular legal topic. For example, suppose you need to research the common law right to privacy. A digest permits you to identify cases that involved an invasion of privacy, over multiple years and jurisdictions. A digest also permits you to find all the cases that have cited a particular statute (unlike an annotated code which provides only some of these cases).

Digests do not set out entire cases. Instead, under each subject in a digest, you will find short summaries known as *headnotes*. These headnotes come from the cases addressing that particular subject. You can use the headnotes to determine whether the case pertains to the issue that you are researching and is, therefore, a case you should read.

The first paragraph in this chapter referred to digest "equivalents." These are search tools that allow topical searching of cases online. Because these online methods are based on the same concepts as print digests, you need to understand how digests are structured even if you do most of your research online.

I. West Digests Generally[1]

This section concentrates on West's digests because they are the most widely used. Much of the information provided here applies to other digests as well.

Most West digests organize cases based on jurisdiction.[2] The digest used for researching Washington law is *West's Washington Digest 2d* (this set is commonly called "*Washington Digest 2d*" or "*Washington Digest*"). It includes headnotes of cases from state and federal courts in Washington, along with cases that originated in Washington and were later decided by the Ninth Circuit Court of Appeals and the United States Supreme Court. This digest also includes citations to some secondary authorities. Figure 6.1 sets out examples of entries from *Washington Digest 2d*.

Some digests index cases from a number of different jurisdictions. For instance, *Pacific Digest* contains headnotes from cases that are reported in *Pacific Reporter* (remember from Chapter 5 that *Pacific Reporter* includes cases from fifteen states). Note that a regional digest like *Pacific Digest* will not include federal cases. Federal cases are included in *Federal Practice Digest*. West also publishes a digest just for United States Supreme Court cases, called *United States Supreme Court Digest*.[3]

Washington Digest 2d replaced the first edition, so it is cumulative, including cases from 1854 to the present. Many other digests are not

---

1. Parts I and II of this chapter are based on materials drafted by Suzanne E. Rowe, editor, Carolina Academic Press Legal Research Series.

2. Some digests are limited by topic, such as *Bankruptcy Digest* and *Military Justice Digest*.

3. Another digest that covers only United States Supreme Court cases is *United States Supreme Court Digest, Lawyers' Edition*. The *Lawyers' Edition* classification scheme for headnotes is not identical to West's system. Be careful not to confuse one publisher's headnotes with those of another.

Figure 6.1 Excerpt from *Washington Digest 2d*
"Torts ☞ 8.5 Invasion of privacy."

8.5(2). Nature and extent of right.

Wash. 1981. Protectable interest in privacy is generally held to involve at least four distinct types of invasion: intrusion; disclosure; false light; and appropriation.
Mark v. Seattle Times, 635 P.2d 1081, 96 Wash.2d 473, certiorari denied 102 S.Ct 2942, 457 U.S. 1124, 73 L.Ed.2d 1339.

Wash. 1947. The "right of privacy" is the right to be let alone.
Lewis v. Physicians and Dentists Credit Bureau, 177 P.2d 896, 27 Wash.2d 267.

Wash.App. 1980. Person's protectable interest in privacy is invaded by unreasonable intrusion upon seclusion or another or into his private affairs, appropriation of other's name of likeness, unreasonable and unwanted publicity given to other's private life or disclosure of embarrassing private facts, or publicity that unreasonably places other in false light before public.
Mark v. KING Broadcasting Co., 618 P.2d 512, 27 Wash.App. 344, affirmed 635 P.2d 1081, 96 Wash.2d 473, certiorari denied 102 S.Ct. 2942, 457 U.S. 1124, 73 L.Ed.2d 1339

Wash.App. 1979. Protection against unreasonable invasion of privacy is main consideration where tort of outrage is asserted against a creditor for his debt collection activities.
Jackson v. Peoples Federal Credit Union, 604 P.2d 1025, 25 Wash.App. 81.

Source: *West's Washington Digest 2d.* Reprinted with permission of West, a Thomson Reuters business. In recent versions of *Washington Digest 2d*, Court of Appeals entries also include the division of the court that heard the case.

cumulative. For example, *Federal Practice Digest 4th* includes headnotes of cases published from the mid-1980s through the present. The previous series, *Federal Practice Digest 3d*, includes cases from 1975 through the mid-1980s. If you are using digests in print, you may need to consult more than one series. Consider the period of time that is pertinent for your research, and then check the introductory information at the front of each print digest to determine whether the digest covers that period. If you are using the digests online, you can limit your search to specific jurisdictions and time periods.

A. Topics and Key Numbers

West digests such as *Washington Digest 2d*, *Pacific Digest*, and *Federal Practice Digest* index cases according to the West system of topics and key numbers. West assigns a topic and key number to each headnote in a case based on the legal point that is the focus of the headnote. The West topic places the headnote within a broad subject area of the law. Examples of West topics include "Criminal Law," "Environmental Law," and "Zoning and Planning." The key number relates to a subtopic within that area of law. An example of a topic and key number for cases dealing with criminal evidence is "Criminal Law 338(2)."[4] The key number "338" refers to subtopic "Relevancy in General," and "(2)" refers to the subheading "Admissibility of Circumstantial Evidence" under this subtopic.

"Criminal Law" is a vast topic, containing more than 1,000 key numbers on subtopics covering criminal intent, defenses, pleas, trials, and sentencing guidelines. A much shorter topic, "Theatres and Shows," includes just a few key numbers on subtopics addressing licenses, admission, and liability for those attending.

B. Headnotes

The digest entries under each topic and key number are identical to headnotes found in cases. West has assigned each headnote a topic and key number. A case is indexed in the digest under as many topics and key numbers as it has headnotes in the reporter.

Each headnote entry contains a sentence summarizing the point of law that relates to the specific subject of the topic and key number

---

4. Some headnotes have parentheses, and some have decimal points. In general, the parentheses are used for subheadings, while decimals are used to insert new key numbers. A topic outline may omit a key number that is no longer used.

assigned to that headnote. Remember that although the language is usually copied directly from the text of the case, headnotes are not authoritative and should never be cited.

In a digest, headnotes are arranged under each topic and key number according to which court decided the case. Federal cases are listed first, followed by state cases. Within these categories, cases are listed according to judicial hierarchy: cases from the highest appellate court are listed first, followed by decisions of intermediate courts, and then trial court cases (remember that selected federal trial court cases are the only trial court cases reported). Cases from each court appear in reverse chronological order from newest to oldest so that you see the cases likely to be most pertinent first.

Although West may have assigned a topic and key number to a particular point of law, a given jurisdiction may not have decided a case on that point. In that instance, no entries appear under the topic and key number of that jurisdiction's digest. However, the topic and key number system makes it easy to research cases in other jurisdictions using West digests, and this may lead to persuasive authorities.

II. Working with Digests in Print

There are several way to research using a print digest. The approach you use depends on what you know when you begin your research, and on what information you need to find.

A. Beginning with a Relevant Case

From reading secondary sources or using annotated codes, you might know a major case on point. Read the case and identify the headnotes that are relevant to your issue. Make a list of relevant topics and key numbers from that case and look them up in a digest that covers the jurisdiction you need; the topics and key numbers are the

Table 6.1 Outline for Digest Research with the
Descriptive-Word Index

---

1. Develop a list of research terms.
2. Find the research terms in the Descriptive-Word Index, which will list topics and key numbers relevant to those terms.
3. Update the Descriptive-Word Index by checking the pocket parts.
4. Review each topic and key number in the main volumes of the digest.
5. Update each topic and key number by checking (1) the pocket part or volume supplement, (2) the cumulative supplementary pamphlet, and (3) the digests in the relevant reporters' most recent advance sheets.
6. Read the relevant cases that your research reveals.

---

same throughout the system. Remember to update your search to find the most recent cases on point.

B. Beginning with the Descriptive-Word Index

Often you will begin your research with a fact pattern and a legal issue, but without any cases on point and without knowing which topics and key numbers may be relevant. In these situations, you will use the Descriptive-Word Index to translate research terms into the topics and key numbers used by the digest to index cases relevant to your client's problem. Table 6.1 outlines this process.

1. Develop a List of Research Terms

Follow the TARPP or journalistic brainstorming method from Chapter 2 to generate a list of research terms that describe the situation you are analyzing.

2. Search the Descriptive-Word Index

The Descriptive-Word Index is contained in several volumes at the end of the digest set. When researching with this index, look

**Figure 6.2 Excerpt from the *Washington Digest 2d*
Descriptive-Word Index Entry "Torts"**

TORTS — Cont'd

POISONS, liability for injuries,
  Poisons ☞ 6

POLLUTION of waters. See heading
  WATER POLLUTION, generally.

PREMISES liability. See heading
  PREMISES LIABILITY, generally.

PRIMA facie torts, **Torts** ☞ 1

PRIVACY, invasion of,
  Generally, **Torts** ☞ 8.5(1–8)
  Consent, Torts ☞ 8.5(8)
  Elements of tort, **Torts** ☞ 8.5(2)
  False light, **Torts** ☞ 8.5(5)
  Speech, freedom of, **Const Law**
    ☞ 90.1(5)
  Intrusion on seclusion, **Torts** ☞
    8.5 (2, 4)
  Nature and extent of right, **Torts**
    ☞ 8.5(2)
  Public figures, **Torts** ☞ 8.5(3, 5)

Source: *Washington Digest 2d*. Reprinted with permission of West, a Thomson Reuters business. Note that if you look up "Invasion of privacy" in the Descriptive-Word Index, there is a cross-reference to see the "Torts" entry.

up your research terms and write down the topic and key number for each term you find. Figure 6.2 shows an excerpt from the entry for "Torts" in the Descriptive-Word Index for *Washington Digest 2d*. Some topics are abbreviated in the Descriptive-Word Index; a list of topics and their abbreviations is included at the front of each index volume.

When you use the Descriptive-Word Index, be sure to record both the topic and the key number. A key number alone is not a helpful research tool. And do not stop looking up research terms after finding just one topic and key number. You should move to the next step only when you have a list of topics and key numbers.

If you do not find any of your terms in the Descriptive-Word Index, brainstorm for additional research terms. If you still cannot find any terms listed, consider moving to a secondary source and coming back to digests once you have learned more about your subject.

3. Update the Descriptive-Word Index

The information included in the Descriptive-Word Index is only as current as the copyright date of that volume. To include new topics and key numbers without reprinting an entire bound volume, the publisher prints pocket parts. To be thorough, you must search the pocket parts for the Descriptive-Word Index for each of your research terms. West publishes pocket parts for the Descriptive-Word Index annually, so if the hardbound volume you are using has been printed within the last year, it will not have a pocket part for you to check.

4. Review Each Topic and Key Number in the Main Volumes of the Digest

Take your topic and key number list to the main digest volumes and find the volume that contains one of your topics. Note that the spine of each digest volume does not list all the topics included in that volume. For example, in the current *Washington Digest 2d*, the topic "Torts" appears in volume 33A. The spine of that volume lists the topics "Telecommunications" to "Trial," indicating that the volume includes those topics and others that come between them alphabetically.

At the beginning of each topic you will find a list of "Subjects Included" as well as "Subjects Excluded and Covered by Other Topics." These lists will help you decide whether that topic is likely to index cases relevant to your research. The list of excluded subjects may contain references to other relevant topics found elsewhere in the digest.

After these lists is the key number outline of the topic, under the heading "Analysis," as seen in Figure 6.3. Longer topics will contain a short, summary outline and then a detailed outline. Many topics follow a general litigation organization, so that elements, defenses, pleadings, and evidence are discussed in that order. Some students find the digest outlines useful when developing course outlines.

You should take a moment to skim the Analysis outline to ensure that you found all the relevant key numbers within that topic. Then turn to each of the relevant key numbers and review the case headnotes there. Write down the citation for each case that you decide you

Figure 6.3 Excerpt from _Washington Digest 2d_ Analysis for "Torts"

II.   PRIMA FACIE TORT.

    151.   In general.
    152.   Constitutional, statutory, and local regulation.
    153.   What law governs.
    154.   Preemption.
    155.   Nature and elements in general.
    156.   Availability of other legal remedy; existence of established tort.
    157.   Intent and malice.
    158.   Justification, or absence or insufficiency thereof.
    159.   Injury or damage from act; causation.
    160.   Balancing of factors or interests.

Source: _Washington Digest 2d_. Reprinted with permission of West, a Thomson Reuters business.

need to read. As with researching in the annotated codes, at this point, the citations that you include in your notes do not have to be complete. They simply need to provide enough information so that you can to find the correct case.

The process of reviewing headnotes and recording possibly relevant cases can be tedious. But your careful review of headnotes is essential. Hurrying through the digest pages will allow you to end your research sooner, but the risk of missing crucial cases is too high.

Nevertheless, you should still be selective in deciding which cases to read. Use the same factors you used in deciding which cases to read from the annotated code (see Chapter 4) in deciding which cases to read from the digests and the order in which to read them.

5. Update Each Topic and Key Number

Like the information in the Descriptive-Word Index, the information in a main volume of the digest is only as current as the volume's publication date. Updated information is most often provided in annual pocket parts. But if the updated information is extensive, the publisher may instead provide a soft bound supplement, normally shelved next to the volume it updates.

When researching in print, be sure that you have found all the cases using your topic and key number, by checking (1) the main digest volumes, (2) either the pocket part or the volume supplement, (3) the cumulative supplementary pamphlet, and (4) the advance sheets. Of course, there will always be some window of time between publication and release of the most current information. For same day currency, you must use an online database. Remember, however, that these digest topics and key numbers are unique to West and work only when you research on Westlaw.

6. Read the Relevant Cases

You must read the cases that you find in your digest search. In fact, your primary task will be to analyze the cases and apply them to your client's situation. Use the strategies for reading cases described in Chapter 5: (1) skim the synopsis and headnotes to see whether the case appears to be on point; (2) find the relevant headnote(s) and turn to that part of the case; (3) skim that portion of the case; and (4) if the case appears relevant, then consider photocopying, printing, or taking notes on it.

Just as with cases you find using the annotated code, with cases you find using the digest, you need to pay attention to how the authorities fit together. Look for trends in the law and pay attention to the facts. Has the law remained stable or have new elements been introduced? Has the meaning of an important term been refined or completely redefined? Does one case summarize the current rule, or do you have to synthesize a rule from several cases, each of which addresses only part of the rule?

C. Beginning with the Topic Analysis Outline

After you have researched a specific area of law many times, you may be familiar with the topics under which cases in that area are indexed. If so, you can begin your research using the Analysis outline that appears at the beginning of each relevant topic. Scan the list of key number subtopics, and then review the headnotes under each key number that appears to be on point. As always, remember to check the pocket parts, supplementary pamphlets, and reporter advance sheets for more recent cases under the topics and key numbers you are searching. Even when beginning research with the topic analysis, it is a good idea to check the Descriptive-Word Index for additional material.

D. Using the Words and Phrases Volumes

To learn whether a court has defined a term, refer to the "Words and Phrases" volumes at the end of the digest set. While *Black's Law Dictionary* will provide a general legal definition of a term, Words and Phrases will direct you to a case that sets out the legal definition of the term in a particular jurisdiction. A judicial definition may be helpful when an important term in a statute is vague and when the statute does not have its own "Definitions" section. A judicial definition can help establish the meaning of a term used in a different context. Figure 6.4 contains an example of a Words and Phrases definition.

Note that entries in Words and Phrases refer to cases that provide judicial definitions of terms, while the entries under topics and key numbers in the main digest volumes refer to cases that discuss, explain, and possibly define a term. The cases listed in Words and

Figure 6.4 Excerpt from Words and Phrases in *Washington Digest 2d*

ANY

Wash. 2002. The word "any" in a statute means "every" and "all." — State v. Westling, 40 P.3d 669, 145 Wash.2d 607. — Statut 199.

Source: *West's Washington Digest 2d.* Reprinted with permission of West, a Thomson Reuters business.

Phrases are thus a specific subset of the cases that appear under related topics in the main digest volumes.

At the end of each entry in the Words and Phrases volumes, West lists the topics and key numbers used for that case's headnotes. The example in Figure 6.4 includes the topic and key number "Statut 199" ("Statut" is the abbreviation for "Statutes").

E. Using the Table of Cases Volumes

The Table of Cases volumes list all the cases indexed in a particular digest series (e.g., *Washington Digest 2d*) by both the primary plaintiff's name and also the primary defendant's name. This table is helpful when you do not know the citation of a relevant case, but do know the name of one or both parties. The Table of Cases provides the full name of the case, the citation for the case, and the relevant topics and key numbers. After consulting the Table of Cases, you can either read the case in a reporter or continue working in the digest using the topics and key numbers to find additional cases.

Alternatively, if you begin your research with a case that does not include West topics and key numbers (for example, you only have access to the case reported in the official Washington reporters), you can use the Table of Cases volumes to learn which West topics and key numbers are used for the case's headnotes. Also, remember that the only online source for cases with West topics and key numbers is Westlaw. You may find the Table of Cases volumes helpful if you do not have access to Westlaw and found a relevant case on another online service.

III. Working with Digests Online

Both LexisNexis and Westlaw provide online digest equivalents. The complete topic and key number outline used by West attorney-editors to classify headnotes is available on Westlaw in the West Key Number Digest, also called the Custom Digest. You can use the West

Key Number Digest to find topics and key numbers related to your issue and to retrieve cases with headnotes classified under those topics and key numbers.

A. Beginning with a Relevant Case

Just as you can begin with a relevant case if you are researching in print, you can also start with one good case if you are researching online.

On Westlaw, if you begin your research knowing one case on point, go to the headnotes in the case that are relevant to your issue. Click on any headnote's key number or on the "Most Cited Cases" link. This will bring up a search box for a custom digest where you can choose a jurisdiction and add search terms. The "Custom Digest" function will find all of the cases with headnotes classified under that topic and key number (and that contain your additional search terms, if any).[5] The cases that are most frequently cited for that point of law will be listed first.

On LexisNexis, you can also use the headnotes to find similar cases. Remember, however, that LexisNexis does not use topic and key number combinations; instead, the system searches for cases that have similar headnotes. At the end of each LexisNexis headnote, click on "More Like This Headnote." This will bring up a search box where you can choose a jurisdiction. The "More Like This Headnote" function will find all the cases in the chosen jurisdiction with similar headnotes.

On both LexisNexis and Westlaw, you can also search for all of the cases that have cited a particular point in your case. On Westlaw, you will use the "KeyCite Citing References for this Headnote" and on LexisNexis, you will use "Shepardize: Restrict By Headnote." Shepard's and KeyCite functions are covered fully in Chapter 7.

---

5. In online searching, each topic is reduced to a number that precedes a "k" and the key number follows. For example, the topic "contracts" is assigned the online number 95. Thus, the topic and key number "Contracts 115" (on restraint of trade) is presented online as "95k115."

B. Using Headnotes for Topical Searching

Both Westlaw and LexisNexis allow searching by topic. In Westlaw, the topical search service is called "KeySearch"; in LexisNexis it is called "Search by Headnote or Topic."

When you access KeySearch on Westlaw (an option at the top of the screen under "Key Numbers"), you will be shown a list of broad topics such as Constitutional Law, Environmental Law, and Intellectual Property. Within these broad topics, you can then select subtopics and a sub-subtopics. For example, to research the liability of a corporation to clean up a polluted lake, click on the topic "Environmental Law," then the subtopic "Water Pollution," then the sub-subtopic "Clean-up Liability." Once you have selected a subtopic (or sub-subtopic) to search, you will need to choose a jurisdiction. Remember to start with the smallest appropriate database (e.g., Washington cases) before widening your search to larger databases. When you run this search, KeySearch identifies the relevant topic and key numbers and other terms based on your choices and constructs a search for cases. In addition, you can add your own terms (using Boolean connectors) to the search. KeySearch retrieves cases as well as documents that do not contain key numbers, such as law review articles and cases without West headnotes.

Searching on LexisNexis with Search by Headnote or Topic is similar. Search by Headnote or Topic has two options. In Option 1, you enter your key research terms to find the topic category that is the closest match. In Option 2, you are presented with an extensive outline of the law, beginning with broad categories similar to the broad categories in KeySearch. You can click on the broad categories to narrow the topic. In either option, once you have narrowed the topic you want to search, a search screen will open. You can link to "analytical materials" such as law reviews or have Search by Headnote or Topic run a case law search. If you run a case law search, you will need to choose a jurisdiction. Like KeySearch, you can either look for all headnotes and additional cases related to your topic or you can add some of your own research terms. Once you have made all of your choices, Search by Headnote or Topic constructs and runs a search based on your topic choices and research terms.

IV. Other Case Finding Strategies

Many new researchers make the mistake of beginning their research by running a terms and connectors search in a case database. This is an inefficient research strategy for several reasons. First, an effective online search is often complex. It is unlikely that early in your research you will know which of your research terms to use and how to connect those terms. Your searches will bring up either too many cases for you to read or too few cases to be helpful. Second, terms and connectors searching is not conceptual searching. When you start with terms and connectors searching, you greatly increase the risk that you will miss related issues because you are looking only for specific words, not more general ideas.

Generally you should wait to search full-text cases until you have a relatively good understanding of the issue that you are researching. You will find that your searches are much less frustrating. Unless you are familiar with an area of law, you should review a secondary source, check the annotated code or digest (or do an online topical search), and read several relevant cases. Then consider running a terms and connectors search in the full text of cases if you think the search will disclose additional authorities.

Because the basic process for doing terms and connectors searching is outlined in Chapter 2, it will only be reviewed here in the context of searching for cases.

First, choose a database. When researching Washington law, start with Washington cases. If you do not find any authority on point, then run your search in a database that includes cases from other states or from federal courts.

Second, generate search terms. You will use the process outlined in Chapter 2, but because you should have already done some research before running the terms and connectors search, you should be able to limit your term list to the most relevant words and phrases.

Third, construct the search using Boolean connectors. Remember that you can expand your search by using less restrictive connectors, and you can perform a "search within your search" by using the "Focus" feature on LexisNexis or the "Locate" feature on Westlaw. Using these features costs less than running a new search.

Fourth, consider restricting your search by West digest topic: use the field restriction (TO) for topic; e.g., TO(privacy). To search for terms used in the headnotes and key number hierarchy, use (DI) for digest; e.g., DI(privacy /s publicity).

The MRSC website (www.legalWA.org) also allows you to perform an "Advanced Search" of case law that is a variation of LexisNexis and Westlaw terms and connectors searching. The website includes boxes for (1) terms you want included in the result cases, (2) terms you do not want included in the result cases, and (3) other search restrictions. Although the searching is a bit more cumbersome than searching on LexisNexis and Westlaw, this website is free and its case database is relatively comprehensive.

The most important thing to keep in mind when using a terms and connectors search to find cases is that finding "more" cases does not necessarily mean that you have performed a more successful search. The cases you retrieve may not be relevant, and you may find that many cases are not applicable and slow down your research process.

You have probably experienced a similar effect when using search engines like Google or Yahoo! When your search yields hundreds of web pages containing your search terms, you probably do not consider all of them relevant, and sometimes the most relevant websites are not the ones listed first. Likewise, an online terms and connectors search for cases that turns up scores of cases probably means that many of them are not relevant. If you are not confident in narrowing down the results, it may mean that you do not yet know enough about your issue to run an effective search. Often, the remedy is more thinking and less searching.

In addition to the strategies discussed above, you will find citators like Shepard's and KeyCite are invaluable case finding tools. Chapter 7 addresses citators in detail.

Chapter 7

Citators

Earlier chapters have discussed how to update cases and statutes using pocket parts, supplements, and databases. This chapter discusses how to update using a *citator*. A citator is a research tool that provides a list of sources that refer to your authority. To illustrate the process of using a citator, this chapter focuses on using a citator to update cases. Citators can also be used to update statutes, constitutional provisions, and secondary sources, processes explained more fully at the end of the chapter.

I. Introduction

Citators have two main purposes. First, a citator helps you determine whether the cases, statutes, and other authorities you want to rely on represent the current "good law." Before using any legal authority to analyze a problem, you must know how that authority has been treated by later action of a court, legislature, or agency. A case may have been reversed or overruled; a statute may have been amended or repealed. Second, because a citator provides a list of citations to sources that refer to your authority, a citator can also be used as a finding tool for cases or other sources. In that sense, a citator works much like a digest or annotated code.

Before using a citator, you need to be familiar with some basic terminology.

Cited source refers to the case, statute, or other authority you are updating.[1]

Prior history refers to what happened to a case before the citation you are updating. For example, the prior history of a Washington Supreme Court case generally would include a citation to the Washington Court of Appeals case that considered the issue before the Supreme Court allowed review.

Subsequent history refers to what happened to a case after the citation that you are updating. For example, the subsequent history of a Washington Court of Appeals case may include a citation to a Washington Supreme Court case reviewing that decision. Unlike prior history, subsequent history can change the precedential value of your case. For example, the Washington Supreme Court often reverses Washington Court of Appeals decisions.

Citing references are the cases and other sources that have cited the case you are updating. A case that cited your case would be a *citing case*. For example, if your cited source was case A, and case A was later referred to in case B, case B would be a citing reference (or a citing case).

Negative treatment means that the citing source may have a negative impact on the validity of your cited source. For example, a citing case may limit the holding in your case by distinguishing the law or facts, or by criticizing the reasoning of the decision.

Positive treatment means that the citing source treated your case favorably. For example, a citing case may follow the holding in your case.

Table 7.1 sets out some of the most common phrases that you will see used to describe how a citing case treats your case.

Treatment flags and *signals* are quick reference tools used by online citators that help you determine the status of a cited source. For example, you may see a red flag, which means that your cited case is no

---

1. *Cited case* refers specifically to a case you are updating. In this chapter, the term "your case" also refers to the case you are updating.

Table 7.1 Common Treatment Phrases

Negative Treatment

Reversed by	The citing case is part of the subsequent history of your case and reversed your case. At least one point of law in your case is not controlling precedent.
Overruled by	The citing case overruled your case, meaning that at least one point of law in your case is no longer controlling precedent.
Distinguished by	The citing case distinguished your case on either the law or its facts.
Criticized by	The citing case disagreed with the reasoning or result of your case.

Positive Treatment

Affirmed by	The citing case is part of the subsequent history of your case and affirmed the decision in your case.
Followed by	The citing case followed at least one of the points of law in your case and cited your case as precedent.

longer reliable authority for at least one point of law in the case. (The different flags and signals used by each citator are described more fully below.) You will also often see a treatment flag or signal when you access a document even when you are not using a citator. For example, if you access a case in Westlaw, you may see a red flag at the top of the page. These flags and signals are based on information from the citator and are a convenient way to link to the citator while you are researching.

Both Shepard's and KeyCite list the status of each case cited in your case, through a *Table of Authorities*. Also both citator systems allow you to track future changes in status by setting up an automatic notification: *Shepard's Alert* and *KeyCite Alert*.

II. Using Citators

Although you can update authorities using print or online citators, this book explains updating using only online citators. Updating in print is a complicated, time-consuming process, and few attorneys use it now that online citators are widely available and relatively inexpensive.

A. Shepard's Online

The first major updating tool was a print resource called "*Shepard's Citations.*" Shepard's was the most widely used method for updating, and some attorneys refer to the updating process as "Shepardizing." LexisNexis now provides Shepard's online.

To access Shepard's, click on the "Shepard's" link at the top of any LexisNexis screen. Type the citation in the Shepard's box provided. For cases, you only need to enter the volume number, reporter abbreviation, and the first page of the case; capitalization and punctuation are optional (e.g., 54 wash app 603).

You can then choose "Shepard's for Validation" or "Shepard's for Research." "Shepard's for Validation" will include (1) subsequent history, (2) citing references that have substantive analysis (i.e., did more than merely cite to your case), and (3) citing references that were added in the last two months. "Shepard's for Research" will include (1) prior and subsequent history and (2) all citing references from cases, statutes, law reviews and periodicals, and other secondary sources. "Shepard's for Validation" is thus a subset of "Shepard's for Research."

1. Using "Shepard's for Validation"

To update your case, choose "Shepard's for Validation." After you press "Check," you will be taken to the result screen. Near the top of the result screen, you will see your case's treatment signal (see Table 7.2). You will see a "Shepard's Summary," which provides an overview

Table 7.2 Shepard's Online Signal Indicators

An online explanation of the signals can be found by using the "Legend" link at the lower left corner of a Shepard's result screen.

Red stop sign	Strong negative history or treatment, e.g., "Overruled by" or "Reversed by"
"!" in a red circle	Warning: Negative case treatment is indicated for statute
"Q" in a yellow box	Questioned; validity questioned by citing sources
Yellow triangle (yield sign)	History or treatment that may have significant negative impact, e.g., "Distinguished by" or "Criticized by"
Green plus sign	History or treatment with positive impact, e.g., "Affirmed by" or "Followed by"
Blue "A"	Treatment that is neither positive nor negative
Blue "I"	Cited in secondary authorities or other sources without history or treatment codes.

Source: "Legend" link at the bottom of Shepard's result screen on LexisNexis.

of the citation analysis. In addition, you will see your case's subsequent history ("Subsequent Appellate History"), followed by the citing cases ("Citing Decisions").

The cases listed in these sections are preceded by phrases that tell you how the subsequent history case or citing case affects or treats your case (e.g., "Reversed by" or "Followed by"). You must read every case listed in the "Subsequent Appellate History" section unless it is a denial of review ("Review denied by"). In addition, you should read any cases listed under "Citing Decisions" that give your case negative treatment to see how they affect your case. As you read, keep in mind the pointers in Table 7.3.

2. Using "Shepard's for Research"

To access "Shepard's for Research," either (1) click on the "Shepardize" option at the top of the case you are using on LexisNexis, or (2)

Table 7.3 Pointers for Reading Negative Cases

- A negative case may have overruled or given other negative treatment to your case only with respect to one issue. If this issue is unrelated to the issue for which you want to use the case, then the case is still good law for your issue.
- You do not necessarily need to read every case from start to finish. Use the hyperlink to go directly to the point in the citing case where it references your case. Read this section before deciding whether to read the entire case.
- If there are too many cases to review, consider looking over only those from your jurisdiction.

---

go back to the Shepard's page and enter your citation into the box, but this time select "Shepard's for Research."

At the top of the result screen is a box titled "Unrestricted Shepard's Summary." The summary box highlights the subsequent history of your case and summarizes the types and number of various citing references (e.g., the number of cases that distinguish your case).

This information is followed by the "Prior History" and "Subsequent Appellate History" of your case. Within the "Prior History" section, the case you entered will be highlighted in blue; this placement shows you where in the litigation process your case occurred. The "Citing Decisions" section is after these history sections. Cases in this section are organized by jurisdiction and court and then listed in reverse chronological order (most recent first). As in "Shepard's for Validation," cases in the history and "Citing Decisions" sections are preceded by phrases that tell you how the case affects or treats your case.

Following the "Citing Decisions" are any annotated statutes that reference your case and then secondary sources.

Often there will be too many cases listed under "Citing Decisions" to read. There are a few ways to determine which ones to look at. First, focus on cases that have substantive analysis (e.g., "Explained by") rather than cases that merely cited ("Cited by") your case.

Next, consider limiting the citing references using Shepard's restriction options. The links to these restrictions are found at the top of the Shepard's result page. You can view only the sources that have given your case negative treatment ("All Neg") or that have given your case positive treatment ("All Pos"). You can use the "FOCUS—Restrict By" feature to run a terms and connectors search within your Shepard's results. In addition, you can use a "FOCUS—Restrict By" option to view cases based on jurisdiction, analysis code, or date. Generally, you should read more recent cases and cases from your jurisdiction first.

You can also use the "FOCUS—Restrict By" option to limit your result by headnote number. If you limit your result in this way, Shepard's will return only citing cases that discuss the point of law represented by the headnote you choose. This type of restriction is particularly useful because it allows you to zero in on the cases that have addressed the issue relevant to your research. Remember not to rely too heavily on the judgment of Shephard's editors. You are responsible for analyzing the cases independently to determine their relevance to the issue you are researching.

When restricting Shepard's results to certain headnotes from Washington cases, you can choose the headnotes from either the official reporter (*Washington Appellate Reports* or *Washington, 2d Series*) or the unofficial reporter (*Pacific Reporter*). Remember that headnote content and numbering differs between the reporters, so make sure you are selecting the headnote numbers from the correct reporter.[2]

Finally, remember that you do not need to read each case from start to finish initially. Skim the synopsis and the headnotes, and look

---

2. In addition to restricting the result list to cases that discuss a point of law from a specific headnote, you can also view your entire result list along with the headnote numbers discussed in each case. Turn on this function using the "Display Options" link near the top of the page. When viewing the entire result list with headnote numbers, the numbers correspond to the headnotes in the reporter that you entered. For example, if you enter a "Wash. 2d" citation, the headnotes will be those from *Washington Reports, 2d Series*.

at the part of the opinion where your case is cited. Then decide if you should read the entire case.

B. KeyCite

Westlaw's citator is called KeyCite. To use KeyCite, log onto Westlaw and click the "KeyCite" link near the top of the page. Once you are on the KeyCite page, enter the citation for your case into the box on the left side of the screen. As with Shepard's, the only part of the citation you need to enter is the volume number, reporter abbreviation, and the first page of the case. With KeyCite, spaces, capitalization, and punctuation are optional (e.g., 54washapp603).

You can also access KeyCite directly from the opening Westlaw page. The opening page is divided into two frames; inside the left frame there is a KeyCite box where you can enter your citation.

After you have entered your citation, the next screen will be divided in half. The left side of the screen has links that allow you to view different parts of your KeyCite results.[3] The right side of the screen contains the information corresponding to what you have chosen in the left side. A blue arrow in the left frame indicates which part of the KeyCite result you are viewing in the right frame. For example, as explained below, the two result lists you can view are "History" (for updating your case) and "Citing References" (to do additional research).[4] At the top of both frames, you will see the treatment flag for your case. Table 7.4 explains what the flags mean.

---

3. This is the same left screen that you see when you view a case on Westlaw. Thus, a third way to access KeyCite is through these links. Using the links in the left frame when viewing a case or statute will change the information in the right frame from your case or statute to the KeyCite information.

4. "History" and "Citing References" are similar to "Shepard's for Validation" and "Shepard's for Research." Nevertheless, there are some important differences. The Appendix to this chapter contains a table illustrating the differences between the kinds of information in each citator.

Table 7.4 KeyCite Status Flags for Cases

An online explanation of the flags in the right frame can be found when you first access KeyCite.	
Red flag	The case is not good law for at least one point (note that it may be authoritative on other points).
Yellow flag	The case has some negative history, but has not been reversed or overruled.
Blue "H"	The case has some history, but it is not known to be negative history.
Green "C"	The case has citing references, but no direct or negative indirect history.

Source: Right frame of main KeyCite page on Westlaw.

1. Using KeyCite to Update a Case

The default view of a KeyCite result is "Full History," which is the view you generally want to use when updating a case. "Full History" includes two categories: "Direct History" and "Negative Citing References." "Direct History" is a chronology of your case through the appellate process (i.e., prior and subsequent history of your case). You can tell where your case fits into the litigation history by the small blue arrow that appears next to its citation. For example, if you KeyCite a Washington Court of Appeals case that was affirmed by the Washington Supreme Court, "Direct History" would show citations to both cases, with a blue arrow next to the Court of Appeals case. As in Shepard's, the entries are preceded by a word or phrase that explains how the entry affects your case. You must read every subsequent history case listed under the "Direct History" section unless it is a denial of review ("Review denied by").

The second category under "Full History" is "Negative Citing References." This section lists the cases that may have a negative impact on the precedential value of your case. For example, "Negative Citing References" will include any cases that overruled your case. A word or phrase in italics before the citation will tell you how the citing case treats your case (e.g., "Overruled by"). If there are cases listed under "Negative Citing References," generally you should read all of them to analyze how they impact your case. However, when reading the cases, keep in mind the pointers listed in Table 7.3.[5]

2. Using *KeyCite* to Do Additional Research

KeyCite can also be used as a case finding tool, and is accessed by clicking on the "Citing References" link below the "History" link. This link will bring up a list of all of the cases, administrative decisions, secondary sources, and briefs and other court documents that have cited your case. Unlike "Shepard's for Research," "Citing References" does not list annotated statutes that have cited your case. "Citing References" first lists the cases that gave your case negative treatment. The remaining cases are listed according to their number of *depth of treatment* stars (see below). After the cases, KeyCite lists other citing references, such as secondary sources.

Often "Citing References" lists too many cases to read. As with Shepard's, there are a few ways to determine which ones deserve attention.

First, KeyCite uses depth of treatment stars to indicate how much "airtime" your case received in the citing cases. The deepest level of treatment is "Examined" and is represented by four stars. The shallowest level of treatment is "Mentioned" and is represented by one star. Generally, focus on cases that have more stars.

Second, after a citation to a case, KeyCite includes a list of headnote numbers. These headnote numbers correspond to headnotes in your case. As with the headnote numbers in Shepard's, these numbers tell you that the citing case discusses the legal issue in that headnote. Generally, focus on cases that have headnote numbers corresponding to the issue you are researching. In KeyCite, the headnote

---

5. KeyCite includes an additional piece of information for the negative history cases and the other citing references. If an entry in your KeyCite result has a set of quotation marks at the end, the case or other authority directly quotes from your case.

numbers correspond to the headnotes in the *Pacific Reporter* (e.g., P.2d), not the official reporter (e.g., Wash. 2d). Unlike in Shepard's, you cannot choose to view the headnotes from the official reporter.

As in Shepard's, you can limit the result to certain types of sources that have cited your case. At the bottom of the screen is a link to "Limit KeyCite Display." You can limit your KeyCite result list based on headnote, date, jurisdiction, document type (e.g., cases or secondary sources), or depth of treatment. As a general rule, read cases that are more recent, from your jurisdiction, and that have the most stars first. You can also use the "Locate" limitation to run a terms and connectors search within your KeyCite results (similar to using the "FOCUS" restriction in Shepard's).

Finally, as noted in the previous section, determine the potential relevance of a case before reading it from start to finish. Skim the synopsis and the headnotes and look at the part of the opinion where your case is cited to decide if you should read the entire case.

III. Evaluating Citator Results

When you read citing sources, you need to decide whether they address the legal question at issue. If a source analyzes only issues that are not relevant to your client's situation, disregard it. If a source is on point, analyze its impact on your case: Does this new source change the rule announced in your case, either by reversing it or overruling it? Or does it follow your case by simply restating the rule and applying it to a similar fact pattern? Does the new source distinguish or criticize your case? If so, how?

Reading the sources you found in a citator will help determine whether your case is good law. It may also lead you to cases in which the court's reasoning is explained more fully or in which the court addresses facts more similar to yours. As you read more and more of these cases, you will be able to identify cases that courts cite most frequently and discuss most fully when addressing your legal issue. Generally, these cases should form the basis of your analysis. You will also see cases that have not been cited or discussed in many later cases.

Generally, these cases may be excluded from your analysis unless the facts are very similar to yours or the reasoning is especially relevant. If you find a line of cases criticizing or distinguishing your case, make sure you address these cases in your analysis.

IV. General Tips

A. Citators' Place in the Research Process

Some researchers wait until late in the process to update their cases so they can update all of them at once. Other researchers update important cases as soon as they find them. A combined approach is often best. Consider updating right away any cases that have a red flag or signal, and updating the rest later. If you have found a "good case," though, do not hesitate to use a citator at any stage of the process to find additional authorities. Often, one good case can lead you to many more.

Finally, be sure to update every authority you are relying on right before you turn in the memo or brief. Both LexisNexis and Westlaw have developed automated cite-validation tools to help with this final check: Shepard's BriefCheck and WestCheck.

Shepard's BriefCheck identifies legal citations in your document, validates these citations through Shepard's, and generates a summary report that highlights problematic citations. To access BriefCheck, click on the "Shepard's" link at the top of any LexisNexis screen and then select the Shepard's BriefCheck link. This will launch BriefCheck. You will be prompted to upload a document or type in a list of citations. BriefCheck will extract the citations from your document and then run a check on them. To return to LexisNexis, simply click on the Lexis.com link in the upper righthand corner.

WestCheck serves the same function as BriefCheck and generates similar reports. WestCheck (www.westcheck.com) is a separate web-based tool that is not directly linked on Westlaw. You can use WestCheck to check citations in KeyCite; to create a table of authorities for cases, statutes, and other legal authority cited in your document; and to retrieve the documents on Westlaw. As in BriefCheck, you will be prompted to upload a document or type in a list of citations. WestCheck will extract citations and quotations from your document and run a check on them.

B. Assessing Flags and Signals

As this chapter has discussed, KeyCite and Shepard's include treatment flags (KeyCite) and treatment signals (*Shepard's*). You will see these flags and signals when you view a case online and when you use the citators. The flags and signals are a quick reference tool that helps you decide whether your case is still good law. But you must not rely on them uncritically. Although a red or yellow symbol may appear because a later court gave your case negative treatment, the negative treatment may not be related to the issue you are researching. Moreover, the many yellow and red symbols you see show a cautious approach by LexisNexis and Westlaw. Knowing that busy attorneys may rely on the symbols, the editors tend to indicate even slightly negative treatment. For these reasons, you need to do your own analysis of the citing references to determine if they truly have a negative impact on your cited source. Finally, although no red flag or signal may appear when your case has been affirmed on appeal, the higher court may have used different reasoning than the lower court. Sometimes courts move away from reasoning in previous cases without indicating this explicitly, and KeyCite or Shepard's editors may not notice the shift. Only a careful reading of the subsequent history will reveal these shifts.

V. Updating Other Authorities

In addition to using a citator to update or research cases, you can also use a citator with many other authorities. For example, you can Shepardize and KeyCite statutes, constitutional provisions, court rules, administrative decisions, and some secondary sources.

Using a citator with statutes deserves special mention. Chapter 4 described how to update statutes online using clues (such as a flag or a bold "Status" line) that you see when you retrieve a statute. These clues are based on information from the citator. If you enter a statute's citation directly into a citator, you will see a history of the statute, i.e., links to session laws that enacted the statute and new session laws amending the statute, and a list of citing references. The list of citing references will often include cases that were not included in the annotated code. This is because a citator contains every source that has cited to the statute; an annotated code is further restricted to those citing sources that the code's editors believed were relevant to the interpretation or application of the statute. Thus, if you do not find enough cases using the annotated code, try using a citator.

As with cases, be careful about relying on flags or signals to tell you the status of a statute. You need to analyze each citing source carefully to determine its effect on the authority you are researching.

VI. Ethical Obligation to Update

Lawyers have an ethical obligation to update their research. Remember from Chapter 1 that the Washington Rules of Professional Conduct require that an attorney provide competent representation, which "requires the legal knowledge, skill, thoroughness and preparation reasonably necessary for the representation."[6] Failing to cite current law or to disclose adverse authority may result in sanctions, malpractice suits, public embarrassment, and damage to your reputation.[7] Mastery of citators can help you avoid these pitfalls.

---

6. RPC 1.1.
7. See Mary Whisner, *When Judges Scold Lawyers*, 96 Law. Libr. J. 557-70 (2004).

Appendix: Table of Selected Differences Between Shepard's and KeyCite

	Shepard's	KeyCite
Validating your case	"Shepard's for Validation"	"History"
	Shepard's for Validation lists (1) subsequent history, (2) citing references that have substantive analysis (i.e., did more than merely cite your case), and (3) citing references that were added in the last two months.	History lists "Direct History" and "Negative Citing References." Direct History is a chronology of your case through the appellate process (i.e., prior and subsequent history of your case). Negative Citing References lists the cases that may have negative impact on the precedential value of your case.
Doing additional research	"Shepard's for Research"	"Citing References"
	Shepard's for Research lists (1) prior and subsequent history, and (2) all citing references from cases, statutes, law reviews and periodicals, and other secondary sources. Shepard's for Research uses treatment phrases such as "Distinguished by" and "Followed by" for all cases.	Citing References lists all of the cases, administrative decisions, secondary sources, and briefs and other court documents that have cited your case. Citing References uses treatment phrases such as "Distinguished by" only for negative cases; "depth of treatment" stars are used for positive cases.
Organizational differences	Shepard's organizes cases by jurisdiction. Shepard's permits you to change the default settings under "Preferences." Shepard's includes a positive treatment signal.	KeyCite organizes cases by treatment and then depth of analysis. KeyCite helps determine how deeply other cases have analyzed your case (depth of treatment stars). KeyCite identifies cases that quote your case (quotation marks).

Chapter 8

Administrative Law

I. Introduction

Administrative law encompasses the regulations (also called rules) and decisions of government agencies. The most common agencies with which administrative law is concerned are those created by statute to accomplish legislative policies, such as the Growth Management Hearings Board, the Utilities and Transportation Commission, and the Department of Licensing. Administrative agencies create detailed sets of rules to administer the programs for which they are responsible. These rules often interpret or fill gaps in statutes. In addition, many administrative agencies create a quasi-judicial process to help them adjudicate disputes arising from the implementation of their rules or enforcement of statutes. Like statutes and cases, administrative agencies' regulations and decisions are primary legal authority.

Each branch of government has some oversight of agency functions. The legislative branch generally delegates to agencies the power to perform their duties through *enabling statutes* and provides funding for the agencies to operate. The legislature also enacts statutes that determine the manner in which the agency can exercise its power. The executive branch oversees most agencies. It has input in the budget process. Moreover, the Governor controls the appointment (and removal) of some agencies' highest officials and may affect agencies by reorganizing some parts of the executive branch. Finally, courts exercise oversight over agencies by interpreting and applying relevant constitutional provisions and statutes, and may determine, among other things, whether agencies' regulations are valid or whether an agency's actions are within the scope of its power.

Administrative law is unique because agencies perform functions of all three branches of government. First, agencies write regulations that interpret and apply statutes; these regulations are similar in form and authority to statutes enacted by the legislature. Second, as a part of the executive branch, agencies issue licenses, conduct investigations to see whether laws are being followed, and enforce laws by imposing civil fines and other sanctions. Finally, agencies also hold quasi-judicial hearings, deciding cases that involve the agencies' regulations or mission. These hearings are similar to court proceedings but are, in some respects, less formal.

In general, agencies function within the bounds of an Administrative Procedure Act (APA), such as Washington's APA, RCW 34.05.[1] Like other administrative procedure acts, Washington's APA specifies the requirements that agencies must follow when adopting a regulation or issuing an adjudicative decision. With respect to both these areas, the principal purposes of Washington's APA are to ensure fairness in administrative processes and to "provide greater public and legislative access to administrative decision making."[2]

II. Administrative Regulations

As noted above, administrative agencies promulgate *regulations* (or *rules*). These regulations may be substantive or procedural. Many regulations supply details that the legislative branch is not able to include in statutes. Because agencies have expertise in particular areas, they are well suited for supplying specific details to general statutes. Regulations may also provide guidance based on an agency's specialized understanding of a relevant statute (or substantive area). Or regulations may determine procedural deadlines and the format for agency filings.

Administrative regulations are written in a format similar to statutes, with outline numbering, and so will look familiar to anyone who has spent time reading statutes. Washington regulations are des-

---

1. Some agencies are exempt from the APA. *See* RCW 34.05.030.
2. RCW 34.05.001.

Table 8.1 Example of Washington Administrative Regulation Numbering

The regulations of the Department of Licensing are contained in Title 308 of the *Washington Administrative Code.* Examples of some of the chapters under Title 308 include the following:

Chapter 308-12	Architects
Chapter 308-20	Cosmetology—Barber—Manicurist—Esthetician rules
Chapter 308-48	Funeral directors and embalmers
Chapter 308-87	Limousine carrier businesses
Chapter 308-104	Drivers' licenses

Within Chapter 308-104, Section 308-104-010 sets out vision test requirements. Similarly, within Chapter 308-20, Section 308-20-120 sets out examination requirements for cosmetologists, barbers, manicurists, and estheticians.

ignated by a three-part number with hyphens separating the parts. The first set of numbers is the agency title number; all regulations issued by an agency are grouped together under the same title, and agencies are arranged roughly in alphabetical order. The second set of numbers represents the chapter number; regulations on the same subject matter within each title are grouped together under the same chapter number. The final set of numbers represents the section number. Table 8.1 shows an example of administrative regulation numbering.

III. Researching Washington Administrative Regulations in Print

A. *Washington Administrative Code*

The State publishes Washington's administrative regulations every other year in the *Washington Administrative Code* (WAC). In the years that the WAC is not published, a supplement is issued. Like the RCW, which codifies (groups by subject) statutes, the WAC codifies regulations. However, unlike the RCW, the WAC has no annotated edition.

There are several ways to determine whether an administrative regulation affects the legal issue that you are researching. One good way is to look for references in one of the annotated statutory codes (the RCWA or the ARCW). In the annotated code, go to the start of the chapter under which your statute falls. If there are related regulations, you will usually see a section entitled "Administrative Code References" (RCWA) or "Washington Administrative Code" (ARCW). Although this section will generally refer to the applicable regulations, often the citation will only be to the WAC chapter where the regulations begin. You will need to browse through all of the WAC sections in that chapter to see if any sections are on point. You may see a reference to an entire WAC title, which means you should look through all of its chapters to see if any regulations are on point. If you do not find regulation references at the statute's chapter level, also check for references at the beginning of the statute's title.[3]

The annotated codes do not always provide a complete list of the regulations relevant to a particular statute. For that reason, you may also want to use the index to the WAC to find relevant regulations. The index for the WAC is not very detailed, and many of the entries are by agency name. This means that using the index will be most helpful when you already know the agencies involved in the area of law you are researching. If you already know the agency name, you can also go directly to the appropriate WAC title and browse through the chapters to see if any of them are on point (the third way to find relevant regulations).

Finally, if you start your research in a secondary source (discussed in Chapter 3), the secondary source will probably cite the applicable regulations.

After finding references to a relevant regulation, read the regulation carefully. Many techniques used for reading statutes apply equally

---

3. Occasionally you may also see regulation references at the individual section level.

to reading administrative regulations. For example, always look for a separate regulation that provides definitions. Also, focus on the text of the regulation, and think about how the conventional tools of statutory construction might apply.

After the text of each regulation appears the history of that regulation. The history is important for determining when the regulation was promulgated, amended, or renumbered. Generally, the regulation that was in effect when the issue you are researching arose will control. For that reason, you may need to read the history note to learn of any changes to the regulation since that time. The historical information includes not only the effective date of the regulation and any amendments, but also the agency's statutory authority for issuing the regulation and any amendments.[4]

Historical information about regulations is listed in reverse chronological order, so look at the effective date of the most recent entry. If your issue arose after this date, you generally do not need to find an earlier version of the regulation. If your issue arose before this date, you would want to find the earlier version. Your law library will probably have the older WAC volumes, or you can use the *Washington State Register* (described below) to find the previous versions.

Just as you need to update statutes, you need to update regulations. Updating regulations is a two-step process. First, check the supplement if there is one. Next, determine whether there have been any changes since the supplement was published by using the *Washington State Register*.

B. *Washington State Register*

Updates to Washington regulations are published in the *Washington State Register* (commonly called the "*Register*"). The *Register* is published on the first and third Wednesdays of each month and is similar to the *Laws of Washington* (or session laws). Like the *Laws of*

---

4. The Code Reviser's office (which publishes the WAC) did not start including the effective date until the late 1980s. For earlier entries, all that is included is the date the final regulation was filed with the Code Reviser.

Washington, which publishes statutes chronologically as the legislature enacts them, the *Register* publishes regulations chronologically as agencies promulgate them.

To update a regulation, you should first check any WAC supplement. Next, go to the most recent issue of the *Register* and check the "Table of WAC Sections Affected" (the table has its own section near the end of each issue). This table is cumulative for the calendar year (i.e., it shows changes in regulations since January of the current year).

If there is a change to your section, the table will refer to the place in the *Register* where you can find the new regulation. Like regulations in the WAC, documents in the *Register* have a three-part number, although the *Register* number is not related to the WAC number. In a *Register* number, the first and second sets of digits tell you the year and the issue number of the *Register* where the document appears. The third number tells you when the document was filed for *Register* publication. For example, if the most recent historical entry includes the number "03-14-046," this means that you can find the amendment in the 2003 *Register*, issue number 14. The document was the 46th document filed for that issue.

To find a previous version of a WAC section, you can use the *Register* citations in the section's history notes. The *Register* entry will show you how the language changed and provide useful background information.

In addition to providing the updated text of regulations, the *Register* gives notice of proposed action on regulations by various agencies. Under Washington's APA, agencies must announce when they intend to introduce new regulations or to modify existing regulations, and the *Register* includes information about when the agency will hold hearings on the proposed regulations and how to submit comments. The *Register* contains other types of information as well, such as executive orders of the Governor.

Register issues are divided into eight sections, each with a different type of information. For example, there is a section containing permanent (final) rules and a section containing proposed rules. Within each individual section, documents are in numerical order based on the third number in the document's *Register* citation.

IV. Researching Washington Administrative Regulations Online

Both LexisNexis and Westlaw have databases containing the WAC. In addition, you can access the WAC on the MRSC website (www.legalWA.org) and on the legislature's website (www.leg.wa.gov/legislature), under the link "Find Laws & Rules." You can search the WAC on the legislature's page (http://apps.leg.wa.gov/wac) by title, by citation, or by term.

When searching for regulations online, you can use some of the same processes as in print. First, after you find a relevant statute, go to the start of the chapter under which it falls (use the "Table of Contents" view). In Westlaw, the first hyperlink under the chapter name is "References and Annotations" for the entire chapter. When you click on this link, you will find the same type of regulation reference that you would find in the print statute (usually a citation to where the related regulations begin in the WAC). On LexisNexis, there is no additional link at the start of each chapter. Instead, the regulation reference will appear at the end of the text of the first section in the chapter.[5]

The hyperlinks in both LexisNexis and Westlaw may not point to the precise section in the WAC because often the regulation reference is to the chapter (or title) where the regulations begin. Nevertheless, you can use the citation given to find the regulations using the online WAC table of contents. As with print research, browse through all of the WAC section or chapter names to see if any of the regulations are on point.

---

5. As with the print versions of the annotated codes, if you do not find administrative code references at the chapter level, also check at the title level. On Westlaw, click on the hyperlink directly below the title name; in Lexis-Nexis, click on the first statute section in the title.

If you already know (or have a good idea of) the relevant agency's name, a second way to find regulations is to go directly to the online WAC table of contents. Expand the appropriate WAC title, and then browse through the title's chapters to see if any of them are on point.

Finally, while you cannot access a WAC index online, online searching does allow you to do a terms and connectors search of the full text of the regulations. Although running a terms and connectors search is not a particularly effective method for finding statutes, it can be an effective method for finding regulations. Regulations tend to be more specific than statutes, and therefore are more likely to contain your particular research terms.

Although online versions of the WAC will be more current than the print version, you will still need to update any applicable sections. Always check the scope of the database you are using (click on the "i" next to the name of the database) to see when it was last updated.

LexisNexis has a database with the *Register*, but the easiest place to update any regulation (even when you use the print version) is on the legislature's website.[6] Click on the link for "Laws and Agency Rules," and then the link for the *Register*. Once you access the *Register* page, you can use the "WAC-WSR Table" (this stands for *Washington Administrative Code* to *Washington State Register* Table). This table is similar to the sections affected table in the print version, except you can use the hyperlinks to go directly to the documents in the *Register* that may affect your WAC section.

V. Judicial and Agency Decisions

Sometimes a research question will require you to find relevant judicial or agency decisions. The best way to find relevant judicial decisions is often to use digests, digest-equivalents, or an online terms

---

6. Note that the Statute Law Committee has declared that the *Washington State Register* published on the Code Reviser's website is the official publication of the Register. *See* http://apps.leg.wa.gov/documents/laws/wsr/ officialstatement.htm.

and connectors search that includes the WAC number as a search term. Since there is currently no annotated version of the WAC, finding judicial decisions relevant to a particular agency rule is more difficult than finding decisions relevant to a statute. However, many of the judicial decisions listed in the statutory annotations will discuss related regulations and so provide an acceptable starting point.

There is no uniform method for finding an agency's decisions. Instead, the research method you choose depends on the agency's structure and how it reports its decisions. Not all agency decisions are readily available, and the format (i.e., print or electronic) varies between agencies. The availability of agency decisions is changing, however, with more information becoming available online. If you need to locate agency decisions, the best place to check is the agency's website (discussed below) or the Internet Legal Resources page maintained by the University of Washington Law Library (http://lib.law.washington.edu/research/research.html). This resource page, which the library updates regularly, has links to administrative decisions and related materials.

In addition to these free resources, LexisNexis and Westlaw have databases with Washington administrative decisions. To see which decisions are available on LexisNexis, look in "Agency & Administrative Materials" under the Washington tab. On Westlaw, look in "Agency & Executive Materials" under Washington materials in the Directory.

VI. Other Agency Resources

The most valuable resource in administrative law research is the agency itself. While statutes and regulations are relatively easy to find, decisions and additional guidelines are more difficult to locate. As mentioned above, one of the best places to find agency decisions is the agency's website; in addition, the agency's website will also provide information about how the agency operates and how to contact the agency. The State of Washington website, Access Washington (http://access.wa.gov) has links to all of the agencies.

Administrative law is complex, and this chapter has barely scratched the surface. If you discover during your research that you are faced with an administrative law issue, you should consult a secondary source. Chapter 3 discusses secondary sources in general and how to find them, but you should be aware that several secondary sources specifically focus on Washington administrative law. One of the best sources is *Washington Administrative Law Practice Manual*, written by the Administrative Section of the Washington State Bar Association and published by Matthew Bender, a member of the Lexis-Nexis group.

VII. Attorney General Opinions

The Attorney General (AG) is the State's lawyer and serves as the constitutional legal adviser to state agencies. In that role, the Attorney General provides formal written opinions ("AGOs") to the State that resemble an attorney's advice to a client, and fall within the general category of administrative law decisions. AGOs respond to specific legal questions from statewide elected officials, members of the legislature, appointed heads of state agencies, and county prosecuting attorneys. For example, a senator may ask about the impact of a statute if enacted, or a prosecutor may ask how an enacted statute applies in a given situation. The opinions establish policy for the AG's office. While legal interpretations in AGOs are not binding, courts give them great weight.

AGOs are designated with a year and a number. For example, AGO 2003 No. 11, responded to a question by Representative Jeff Morris about the authority of cities, towns, and counties to provide telecommunication services to their residents. You may see an opinion designated with "AGLO" instead of "AGO." This simply means the opinion is an attorney general "letter opinion," a type of less widely distributed opinion issued by the Attorney General's office during the 1970s and 1980s.

There are several ways to access AGOs. You will find citations to the opinions as part of the annotations in the RCWA and the ARCW. The opinions themselves are available in print in hardbound volumes. Because there are several indexes, each spanning a certain number of years (e.g., 1965–75), you can search for an opinion even if you do not have a citation.

The opinions are also available online at the Attorney General's website (www.atg.wa.gov). The website has opinions from 1949 to the present and a cumulative index (starting with opinions from 1975) that allows you to look for an opinion by subject. LexisNexis and Westlaw also contain databases with opinions from 1949 to the present.

VIII. Federal Administrative Law[7]

The federal government's agencies function much like Washington's. Agencies such as the Civil Rights Division of the Department of Justice, the Internal Revenue Service, and the U.S. Fish and Wildlife Service represent important parts of the executive branch.

The federal APA is codified at 5 USC §§ 551–559. Like Washington's APA, its goal is to promote uniformity, public participation, and public confidence in the fairness of the procedures used by government agencies.

A. Code of Federal Regulations

Federal regulations are published in the *Code of Federal Regulations* (CFR), which is published by the Governmental Printing Office (GPO). The CFR codifies regulations issued by federal agencies. Like regulations in the WAC, regulations in the CFR are organized by agency and subject. The fifty titles of the CFR do not necessarily correspond to the fifty titles of the United States Code (USC), although some topics do fall under the same title number. For instance, Title 7 in both the CFR and the USC pertain to agriculture, but Title 11 of

---

7. Part VIII is based on materials drafted by Suzanne E. Rowe, editor, Carolina Academic Press Legal Research Series.

the USC addresses bankruptcy while the same title in the CFR deals with federal elections.

CFR volumes are updated annually, with specific titles updated each quarter (e.g., Titles 1 through 16 are updated as of January 1; Titles 17 and 27 are updated as of April 1).[8] But these updates may become available only months after the schedule indicates. Each year, the CFR volumes' covers are printed using a different color, which makes it easy to tell whether a print volume has been updated. If no changes were made in a particular volume for the new year, a cover with the new color is pasted on the old volume.

Federal regulations are available online at the GPO website (www.gpo.gov) and on LexisNexis and Westlaw. The text on the GPO website is no more current than the print versions; the text on Lexis-Nexis and Westlaw is more up to date. Clicking on the scope command next to the name of the database will tell you when the information was last updated.

To research a topic in the CFR, you can use several methods. First, you can look up your research terms or the relevant agency's name in the general index, and then read the regulation referenced. However, it may be more efficient to begin your research by looking at an annotated statutory code, which will often contain cross-references to relevant regulations. Finally, starting your research in a secondary source may also lead you directly to relevant regulations.

B. *Federal Register*

New regulations and proposed changes to existing regulations are published first in the *Federal Register*, the federal equivalent of the *Washington State Register*. The *Federal Register* is the first print source to publish regulations before they are adopted (i.e., before they are codified in the CFR). In addition to providing the text of regulations,

---

8. The exception is Title 3, "The President," which includes executive orders. Unlike other CFR titles, each annual volume of Title 3 is a unique source of Presidential documents and must be retained to provide access to executive orders still in effect.

the *Federal Register* also contains notices of hearings, responses to public comments on proposed regulations, and helpful tables and indexes. It is published almost every weekday, with continuous pagination throughout the year. This means that page numbers in the thousands are common. An online version of the *Federal Register* is available on the GPO website and on LexisNexis and Westlaw.

C. Updating Federal Regulations

To update a federal regulation in print or on the GPO website, begin with a small booklet or the online database, both of which are called the *List of CFR Sections Affected* (LSA). As its name suggests, the LSA lists all sections of CFR that have been affected by recent agency action. The LSA provides page references to *Federal Register* issues where action affecting a section of CFR is included. If the section you are researching is not listed in the LSA, then it has not been changed since its annual revision. The LSA is published monthly, so you will also need to do final updating to check for changes since the most recent version of the LSA.

Final updating of federal regulations in print requires reference to a table at the back of the *Federal Register* called "CFR Parts Affected During [the current month]." (Do not confuse this table with the daily update "CFR Parts Affected in this Issue" located at the beginning of each issue.) Refer to this table in the *Federal Register* for the last day of each month between the most recent monthly LSA issue and the current date. Also check the most recent issue of the *Federal Register* for the present month.

To do your final updating on the GPO website, you need to check a database called "Current List of CFR Parts Affected," which will indicate any changes in the regulations during the current month. If the LSA for the previous month has not yet been issued, the website will also post "Last Month's List of CFR Parts Affected."

To update a federal regulation in LexisNexis or Westlaw, search the *Federal Register* database using the name of the agency that issued your CFR section and a date restriction as your search terms. You should use the name of the agency that issued the CFR section instead of the section number because a new regulation affecting your section may not refer to the section number, but it will always include the agency's name.

D. Decisions of Federal Agencies

Like Washington's agencies, federal agencies hold quasi-judicial hearings to decide cases that arise under the agency's regulations. Some of these decisions are published in government reporters specific to each agency, for example, *Decisions and Orders of the National Labor Relations Board* (NLRB); some are also reported in commercial publications, for example, *Labor Relations Reporter*. LexisNexis and Westlaw both have databases containing decisions of federal agencies, and the website for the agency itself may allow you to access the agency's decisions. The University of Virginia Library hosts a useful site with deep links to federal agency decisions and other actions (www2.lib.virginia.edu/govtinfo/fed_decisions_agency.html).

Chapter 9

Legislative History

This chapter covers the process by which the Washington legislature enacts laws, and it explains how to track pending legislation and research legislative history.

Tracking pending legislation (or *bill tracking*) involves monitoring the status of a current bill in the legislature. Lawyers track bills in a number of different circumstances. For examples, lawyers may need to learn about proposed legislation to advise clients about business decisions. Similarly, when acting on behalf of clients as lobbyists, lawyers need to know about legislative proposals. Less frequently, lawyers can help establish the legislative intent of previously enacted statutes by referring to pending legislation.

In addition to tracking pending legislation, lawyers often need to reconstruct the steps in the legislative process for laws that have already been enacted — or compile a *legislative history*. Legislative history refers to all the documents that are produced during the legislative process: for example, committee reports, amendments, transcripts of floor debate, and executive signing or veto messages. Most often, lawyers use legislative history to better understand the legislative intent or purpose of ambiguous statutes, and to marshal arguments in support of a preferred interpretation.

I. Introduction

The Washington State Legislature consists of two chambers: the Senate, with forty-nine members, who serve four-year terms; and the

House of Representatives, with ninety-eight members, who serve two-year terms. A legislative "cycle" lasts two years, and so each cycle is called a *biennium*. Each biennium has two regular legislative sessions. As mentioned in Chapter 4, regular sessions start in January and last for 105 days in odd-numbered years and 60 days in even-numbered years. In addition, the Governor may call extraordinary (or special) legislative sessions to address specific issues, for example to deal with a fiscal crisis.

The general process of enacting or amending laws in Washington resembles that in other states and the United States Congress. Table 9.1 shows the basic progression of an idea from bill to statute and notes the most important documents that emerge from the legislative process.

Table 9.1 How a Bill Becomes a Law

Legislative Action	Documents Produced
A legislator introduces a bill on the floor (the actual space where each chamber meets) of either the House or Senate. This is called the bill's first reading (even though the entire text of the bill probably will not be read aloud). At the first reading, the bill is assigned to a committee.	The first document produced is the **original bill** itself. Each bill has a **bill digest** (a summary of the bill) and a **bill history** (a list of procedural actions taken on a bill, such as a first reading). The proceedings (e.g., floor action such as the first reading of a bill) of the House and Senate are recorded in their respective **journals**.
The committee studies the bill and may hold public hearings. The committee then decides whether to pass the bill (with or without amendments), present a substitute bill, reject the bill, or take no action at all.	As noted, a committee may propose a **substitute bill**. In addition, as the bill moves through the committee process, the legislative staff produces a **bill report**. The bill report contains background on the issue addressed by the bill, a summary of the legislation, the names of those who testified on the bill, and a summary of the testimony.
If the bill is passed, the full chamber (either the House or Senate) acts on the committee's recommendation (called the committee's "report"), and then the bill is referred to the Rules Committee. The Rules Committee is the committee that sets the chamber's calendar. The Rules Committee can either place the bill on the calendar for a second reading or let the bill die.	A committee's recommendation (e.g., to pass the bill) is called a committee "report"; do not confuse this with a "bill report." Also, remember that each bill has a **bill history** and that each chamber keeps a **journal** of its proceedings. Both of these documents will indicate when there was floor action on the bill, such as reading of the committee report and referral to the Rules Committee.

Table 9.1 How a Bill Becomes a Law, *continued*

Legislative Action	Documents Produced
At the second reading, a bill is subject to debate and amendment before being placed on the third reading calendar for passage.	If a bill has been amended in committee or on the floor in the first house, it is ordered *engrossed*. An engrossed bill has all of the amendments incorporated into the body of the bill. When the first chamber sends the bill to the second chamber, the second chamber then receives a single document.
When the bill has its third reading, the members vote. If the bill passes, it moves to the other chamber where the process above is repeated.	In the second chamber, additional legislative history, of the type described above, is produced.
If the second chamber passes the bill without making any changes, the bill is sent to the Governor for signature. If it is passed with amendments, it goes back to the first chamber for a vote on the changes. If needed, a conference committee is appointed with legislators from both chambers who work out the differences. When the two chambers concur on the final bill, it is sent to the Governor for signature.	Once a bill finally passes both houses, it is *enrolled*. An enrolled bill has amendments from both houses incorporated. After a bill is passed, the legislative staff prepares a final bill report. Note that this means an enacted bill will have three bill reports: a House bill report, a Senate bill report, and a final bill report.
The Governor may sign the bill, veto (in whole or in part) the bill, or take no action. If the Governor does not sign the bill, it becomes law without signature. If the Governor vetoes all or part of the bill, a two-thirds vote in both chambers will override the veto.	The Governor may include a veto message, explaining why he or she did not approve part of the bill.
The enacted bill is assigned a session law number; in Washington, this is called a *chapter number*. This is a chronological number based on when the bill was passed in that session of the legislature.	The Office of the Code Reviser publishes the session laws in the *Laws of Washington*.
The law is codified, meaning that it is assigned a number that places it with other laws on similar topics.	The Office of the Code Reviser codifies the session laws in the *Revised Code of Washington*.

Because the legislature works in a two-year cycle, a bill that does not make it all the way through this process during a single session is not necessarily dead. If the bill was introduced during the first regular session, it will *carryover* to the next session and can be taken up in later sessions of the biennial cycle. The legislative history of a particular bill may therefore span different legislative sessions. If a bill does not make it through the legislative process by the end of the biennium it is considered "dead."

II. Washington Bill Tracking

Bills introduced during a legislative session may propose new laws or amend existing laws, affecting a client's rights. For example, a new law expanding the class of persons protected by employment discrimination statutes could alter the kinds of questions an employer may ask during job interviews. In advising a client, a lawyer must learn of any bills relevant to the client's interests and track the bills' progress through the legislative process. The best place to track bills in Washington is the legislature's own website, which is free and up to date.[1] Table 9.2 outlines the process for bill tracking online.

Table 9.2 Outline for Bill Tracking Online

1.	Go to the legislature's website. This link is available on the State of Washington website (http://access.wa.gov). Click on "Government," and then "Laws & Rules."
2.	Click on the "Bill Information" link; this brings up bill information for the current biennium.
3.	If you know the bill number, simply enter the four-digit number into the search box.
4.	If you do not know the bill number: a. enter a search term into the search box; or b. look for your search terms in the online topical index; or c. use the "RCW to Bill" cross-referencing table.

1. LexisNexis and Westlaw also provide bill tracking services, but this book focuses on the legislature's website because the information is free, easy to access, and current.

A. Researching with a Bill Number

If you have a bill number for the legislation you want to track, you need only type the four-digit bill number into the search box on the legislature's bill search website. This will take you to a bill information page, which describes the bill's history (the committees that considered the bill and when) and links to available documents (such as the different versions of the bill, bill digests or summaries, bill reports, and proposed amendments).

B. Researching without a Bill Number

There are a number of ways to search for pending legislation without a bill number. The legislature's bill information page includes a "Bills By Topic" index, an alphabetical list of subjects addressed by bills from the current biennium that you can view in various ways. For example, if you click on the topic "Animals" you will find all the pending legislation that the Code Reviser's office assigned to that category; in the 2007–2008 biennium, legislation involving animals ranged from bills regarding the certification of animal massage practitioners to consumer protection bills concerning adulterated pet food. The Bills By Topic index includes links to a specific information page for each bill, which includes the information described above.

Instead of using the Bills By Topic index, you can search bill descriptions. This method has certain limitations. First, the search engine does not permit full-text searching of proposed legislation; instead, it searches only one- or two-line bill descriptions. Second, the search engine lacks sophistication and does not currently allow the use of Boolean connectors (e.g., you may have trouble finding bills using more than one word). For these reasons, the Bills By Topic index permits the most efficient and reliable way to search pending legislation when you do not have a bill number.

A final way to search pending legislation when you know a particular section of the *Revised Code of Washington* (RCW) is to use the "RCW to Bill" cross-reference tool. The link to this tool is also on the Bill Information page. This tool lists all RCW sections potentially affected by one or more bills pending before the current legislature.

Bill tracking is also easy to do on Westlaw. When you access the RCWA on Westlaw, KeyCite will flag any pending legislation that may affect your statute. On LexisNexis, you cannot track bills from the RCW. Instead, access the source "Washington Bill Tracking," to monitor the status of pending legislation.

III. Washington Legislative History Research

Legislative history research can shed light on the meaning of an ambiguous statute by providing evidence of the legislature's intent or purpose in enacting that statute. In some sense, legislative history is the reverse of bill tracking. While bill tracking follows the legislative process forward, from the introduction of a bill to its possible enactment, legislative history research works backwards, beginning with an enacted statute and uncovering all the documents produced during its enactment. This section explains the sources of legislative history in Washington and how to conduct legislative history research.

A. Sources of Washington Legislative History

A number of different documents emerge from the legislative process. Look back at Table 9.1 for a reminder about how these documents fit into the legislative process. This section describes the most important documents and briefly discusses their significance.

1. Bills

Bills change as they travel through the legislative process. The various versions (original, engrossed, substitute, and enrolled) of a bill and committee or floor amendments can be important when interpreting statutes because changes to the text of a bill may help determine what the legislature intended or did not intend in enacting it.[2]

Bills usually have a letter component and a number component. The letter component will tell you the chamber in which the bill was introduced. Some common abbreviations in the letter component are "HB" (House bill), "SB" (Senate bill), "E" (engrossed bill), and "S" (substitute bill). You will often see a combination of these letters. For example, "ESHB 5665" would be the abbreviation for an engrossed substitute House bill.

In Washington, the bill number remains the same throughout the process. Sometimes a number designation will appear along with the "S" or the "E." Ordinarily, if the number appears before the "S" (e.g., 2SHB 5665) it means that the bill was sent to more than one committee and more than one committee offered a substitute bill. If the number appears before the "E" (e.g., 2EHB) it indicates the bill was sent back to its original chamber (e.g., it was a carryover bill) and was amended when it was returned.

2. Digests and Histories

Digests and histories are published in the *Legislative Digest and History of Bills*. Remember that a bill *digest* is a short summary of a bill and a bill *history* is a chronological list of all the actions taken on the bill. Bill histories tell you which committees considered the bill and when the bill was amended.

3. House and Senate Journals

As indicated in Table 9.1, the legislative activities of each chamber are recorded in journals, called the *House Journal* and the *Senate Journal*, which are published annually and are available primarily in print form. Electronic copies of the journals are available from 1993 to date. The *Journals* include bill readings, committee "reports," other floor action, and action by the Governor. *Journals* also include colloquies

---

2. The Washington State Legislature provides an online glossary of legislative terms at www.leg.wa.gov/WorkingwithLeg/glossary.htm.

(questions and answers between legislators) and the text of amendments. But the *Journals* do not provide a complete source of legislative history. For example, the *Journals* do not include the text of debates (though they do often indicate that debate occurred). Likewise, the *Journals* also include only the committee's "report" on whether to pass a bill, not the bill report itself. Note that the *Journals* are different from bill histories: bill histories track legislative steps with respect to a single bill, while the *Journals* track all the happenings in the legislative chambers, and typically include information about many bills.

4. Bill Reports

Each enacted bill will have three bill reports: a House report, a Senate report, and a final bill report.[3] House and Senate bill reports are more detailed than final bill reports. As noted in Table 9.1, bill reports contain some legislative history, background information, a summary of the legislation, how the bill was reported by committee, a summary of the testimony in committee, and a list of who testified. The staff updates the bill report as the bill moves through the legislative process.

For bills enacted after 1974, the final bill reports are published in the *Final Legislative Report*. House and Senate bill reports for these bills are kept at the State Archives (discussed in Section B.3). Final bill reports for bills enacted since 1997, are also available on the legislature's website, along with the House and Senate bill reports. For House and Senate bill reports for bills enacted before 1997, you need to contact the State Archives (discussed in Section B.3).

5. Signing or Veto Messages

In Washington, the Governor can issue statements upon signing or vetoing legislation to explain why he or she approved or did not approve a particular bill. These messages can help lawyers or courts understand the meaning of ambiguous legislation. Signing messages

---

3. The House staff also prepares a "House Analysis" for each bill. The House Analysis is prepared prior to any committee work on the bill and contains information similar to that in a bill report.

can indicate the Governor's understanding of the bill, which in turn can provide policy context or hints about the meaning of disputed terms. Veto messages become especially important if a bill that the Governor vetoed is later modified and enacted with the Governor's signature. In such a case, the Governor's veto messages might provide useful background for understanding the scope, purpose, or meaning of the new bill. Signing and veto messages are published in several sources, including the session laws (in the *Laws of Washington*), the final bill report (in the *Final Legislative Report*), and the *Journals*.

6. Session Laws

Session laws have been discussed in several places in this book. When doing legislative history, session laws are important because they will tell you the bill number that you need to research and enable you to retrieve prior versions of a statute. The next section explains how to read the session law citations at the end of a statute.

B. The Research Process

As with other kinds of research, one of the most efficient ways to begin researching legislative history is to see whether any secondary sources have already compiled some of the information you need. Often a case or law review article (or, with luck, a formal legislative history compilation) will contain legislative history information for a statute; see if this information is helpful before undertaking more research on your own.

If you need to do your own research, the first step is to find out when the statute or amendment you are interested in was enacted. The historical information that follows the statute contains this information. At the end of each statute (in the RCW, the ARCW, or the RCWA), you will see a series of citations and dates in brackets. These refer to the session law that was codified in the statute and its date of enactment. The bracketed information will also include references to session laws for any amendments to the statute. Ultimately, you will

Figure 9.1 Excerpt from the *Revised Code of
Washington Annotated*

4.24.210. **Liability of owners or others in possession of land and water
areas for injuries to recreation users — Limitation**

(1) Except as otherwise provided in subsection (3) or (4) of this section, any public or private landowners or others in lawful possession
and control of any lands ... who allow members of the public to use
them for the purposes of outdoor recreation ... shall not be liable for
unintentional injuries to such users.

(2) Except as otherwise provided in subsection (3) or (4) of this section, any public or private landowner or others in lawful possession
and control of any lands ...

(3) Any public or private landowner, or others in lawful possession
and control of the land, may charge an administrative fee ...

(4) Nothing in this section shall prevent the liability of a landowner
or others in lawful possession and control for injuries sustained to
users by reason of a known dangerous artificial latent condition ...

(5) For purposes of this section, the following are not fees ... ;

[2006 c 212 § 6, eff. June 7, 2006. Prior: 2003 c 39 § 2, eff. July 27,
2003; 2003 c 16 § 2, eff. July 27, 2003; 1997 c 26 § 1; 1992 c 52 § 1;
prior: 1991 c 69 § 1; 1991 c 50 § 1; 1980 c 111 § 1; 1979 c 53 § 1; 1972
ex.s. c 153 § 17; 1969 ex.s. c 24 § 2; 1967 c 216 § 2.]

Source: *Revised Code of Washington Annotated.* Reprinted with permission
of West, a Thomson Reuters business.

need to find the legislative history for each amendment that affected
language pertinent to your research. Annotated codes make this task
easier by summarizing amendments to the statute. These summaries
give you a good sense of whether you need to find legislative history
of those amendments.

Figure 9.1 shows an example of a Washington statute and the
bracketed historical information that follows it. The last citation,
[1967 c 216 § 2], means that the law was enacted in 1967 and was assigned chapter number 216. Remember from Chapter 4 that a session
law's chapter number simply indicates when it was passed during the

legislative session. In this case, this means that the session law was the 216th law enacted during the regular session of 1967.[4] This statute is found in section 2 of chapter 216.

The citations to the session laws are usually listed in reverse chronological order. This means that amendments are listed before the original statute; the original enactment of the statute should be at the end of list. You can see that the statute in Figure 9.1 has been amended several times, most recently in 2006. The abbreviation "ex.s." before a chapter number (e.g., in the citation to the 1972 session law in Figure 9.1) indicates that the legislature enacted that session law during a special (extraordinary) session instead of a regular session.

Once you know when your statute or amendment was enacted, you can start the research process. If the legislature passed your bill or amendment in 1992 or later, you can do most of the research online; for bills passed before 1992, you will need to use print materials.

1. Legislative Research Online

a. Using the State's Website

For recent statutes and amendments, you can do most of your research online using the Legislature's website.[5] This will save you considerable time in not having to find the various print sources. The legislature's website gives users a number of different methods to find legislative history. The steps below outline one way to find legislative history for your bill or amendment:

(1) Go to the legislature's homepage (www.leg.wa.gov/ legislature), and choose the "Bill Information" link on the right side. This link brings up bill information for the current bi-

---

4. Do not confuse "chapters" in session laws with the "chapters" in the code; the session law chapter number provides purely chronological record keeping, while the code chapter number places the enacted law in context with other statutes on similar topics.

5. At the time of writing, the legislature's website provided information for bills through the 2009–10 biennium at http://apps.leg.wa.gov/billinfo. Historical bill information, from 1991–92 through 2007–08 was provided at https://dlr.leg.wa.gov/billsummary.

ennium. Links or tabs for previous bienniums are also available.

(2) Once you have selected the biennium during which your session law was enacted, use the "Bill/RCW/Session Law Cross Reference" tool to find the bill number associated with your session law chapter number. Remember that the bill number will also include letter abbreviations; use the abbreviations to determine the chamber in which the bill originated.

(3) As soon as you know the bill number and the chamber in which the bill originated, return to the Bill Information page for the appropriate biennium. If your bill was enacted in 2001 or later (newer bills), enter your bill number into the search box. If your bill was enacted before 2001 (older bills), choose the link at the top of the page for historic bill information.

The legislature presents information in slightly different forms for different bienniums. For newer bills, entering the bill number will bring you to a "Bill Summary" page (just as you would see when tracking a bill). This page includes links to all versions of the bill and amendments, the bill digest and history, any bill reports, and any signing or veto message. The state website has a separate section for older bills. Entries in this section contain some of the information or documents you would find on the Bill Summary of newer bills, but they are not complete.

If the documents you find online do not give you enough information, you may want to consult both the *House Journal* and *Senate Journal* to find out if there were any colloquies or debates. For the most part, you will have to use the journals in print. Electronic copies of both journals from 1993 to the present are available at http://search.leg.wa.gov/advanced/3.0/main.asp. Go to each chamber's last *Journal* volume for the appropriate session. At the back of these volumes, you will find a table of bill numbers and the pages on which there are references to these bills. Check every page reference because you cannot be sure where colloquies or debate references will appear. If your search reveals that there was debate on the bill, you will need to ask the Journal Clerks[6] to send you audiotapes of the debate or you can see if the audio is available online at TVW's website (described in Section B.4).

As a last step, you can also contact the State Archives (or the committee to which the bill was assigned if the bill was introduced within the last two years) to see if there is any additional information in the bill file. The State Archives and bill files are discussed more fully after the section on print research.

b. Using Westlaw and Lexis

Westlaw and LexisNexis now include Washington legislative history documents for recent Washington statutes in their databases. One way to find legislative history on Westlaw is to locate the statute you are interested in and look on the left-hand side of the screen for a heading called "Legislative History." Under this heading, you will see links to documents such as the text of any amendments. If Westlaw has any legislative history documents (such as bill reports, vote records, or Governor's messages), you will see a link to "Reports and Related Materials." Click on this link to view a list of available documents, arranged by session law. You can also search the database WA-LH. LexisNexis allows similar searching of Washington legislative history. You can locate legislative history on LexisNexis by clicking on "Find Statutes, Regulations, Administrative Materials and Court Rules" in the "Look for a Source" box and then by clicking on the "Washington Legislative History Bill" link. LexisNexis bill information begins with 1990.

2. Legislative Research in Print

If your statute was enacted before 1992, you will need to do your research using print resources. The process for doing legislative history research in print is outlined below:

---

6. The Journal Clerks are the staff members responsible for publishing the *Journals*. To contact either the House or Senate Journal Clerk, call the Legislative Information Center Hotline at (800) 562-6000 and ask to be connected to the appropriate clerk.

(1) For print research, you will first need to find out the bill number for the session law by looking up the session law in the *Laws of Washington* (or by using an electronic resource).

(2) Next, go to the volume of the *Final Legislative Report* for the appropriate session and look up the final bill report. At the start of each volume, there is a numerical list of bills that indicates the page number on which the bill report appears. The *Final Legislative Report* will also contain any signing or veto messages for the bill. The *Final Legislative Report* does not contain the House bill report or the Senate bill report; therefore, for bills enacted before 1997, you will need to contact the State Archives for these bill reports.

(3) Next, find the bill's digest and history in the *Legislative Digest and History of Bills*. This will tell you when each reading of the bill occurred, to which committees it was referred, and when it was amended or substituted. Then look at the different versions of the bill. Unfortunately, finding different versions of a bill in print is more difficult than it is online. Some law libraries have copies of old bills, and the State Archives also keeps copies. If you need old bill copies, ask a reference librarian for assistance.

(4) As with online research, you need to check the *House Journal* and the *Senate Journal* for debate references and colloquies. In addition, the *Journals* contain the text of amendments, which may be helpful when doing print research.

If you have not found enough information through these sources, your next step is to contact the State Archives to see if any additional information is available in the bill file.

3. State Archives

The State Archives (www.secstate.wa.gov/archives) is a division of the Secretary of State that collects and stores historical government documents. The Archives collection includes committee meeting tapes and legislative files with documents related to bills introduced from approximately the mid-1970s to the present. Legislative files in-

clude House and Senate *committee bill files*, which contain committee reports, various drafts of the bill, amendments, staff summaries,
and related backup material. In addition, the Archives has House and
Senate *committee meeting files*, which contain rosters of interested
parties who appeared at committee hearings, committee agendas, and
sometimes copies of written testimony on a bill. The Archives collection also includes materials for researching bills enacted before the
mid-1970s.

The State Archives is located in Olympia. If you call the Archives
at (360) 586-1492, the staff will research a bill and copy the committee bill file for a fee. Of course, you can also research the files on your
own, but you still must call ahead and ask the staff to pull the files.
At the time of writing, the State Archives was planning to release digital access to the debates of the Washington State legislature for
1973–92. For more information, see www.digitalarchives.wa.gov.

4. TVW

TVW is a private, non-profit organization that provides video and
audio coverage of state government deliberations and public policy
events. It is similar to C-SPAN on the federal level. TVW's website
(www.tvw.org) has archives of nearly all House and Senate floor debates and committee meetings since 1997 as well as some material
from 1996. You can listen to the streaming audio or video for free, or
you can purchase a recording.

5. Researching Older Statutes

As shown above, the newer the statute you are researching, the easier it will be to find information. For bills enacted before the mid-
1970s, you usually will not be able to find much information. For help
in finding the legislative history for bills enacted before the mid-1970s,
review the research strategies in Part III of Chapter 6 in the *Washington Legal Researcher's Deskbook 3d*, which is listed in Appendix B of this
book. In addition, you should talk to a reference librarian, and you will
probably need to contact the State Archives.

C. The Use of Legislative History in Legal Analysis

When planning or conducting legislative history research, keep in mind that not all judges embrace the use of legislative history, especially when the meaning of the statute in question seems clear. Some judges believe that it is difficult, if not impossible, to determine the intent of a large and diverse group of legislators from documents produced during the legislative process. Before spending time on legislative history research, try to find out whether the court in which you are appearing will find it persuasive given the particular circumstances of your case. In some circumstances, researching legislative history may not be worth the effort.

Moreover, courts do not give all legislative history materials the same weight. Although no Washington case or statute sets out an official ordering of persuasive value, courts and commentators have established a generally accepted hierarchy. At the top is the preamble or purpose statement of an enacted statute. If the legislature expressly adopts a statement of purpose, this is the clearest statement of legislative intent other than the text itself. Official documents such as bill reports are farther down the scale (remember that the reports are prepared by legislative staff, not members of the legislature). Bill drafts, committee work (such as statements of legislators and witness testimony), and floor debates and colloquies come next, followed by a Governor's signing or veto message. The least persuasive source of legislative history is material produced after the legislature enacts the statute.[7]

---

7. The hierarchy described in this paragraph is taken from Philip A. Talmadge, *A New Approach to Statutory Interpretation in Washington*, 25 Seattle U. L. Rev. 179, 204–06 (2001). For a more detailed discussion assessing various forms of legislative history, see William Eskridge et al., *Cases and Materials on Legislation: Statutes and the Creation of Public Policy* (4th ed. 2007).

IV. Initiative and Referendum Research

In addition to the traditional method of enacting law, Washington's initiative and referendum processes allow for direct legislation by the people of Washington.[8]

The initiative process gives voters the power to enact new laws or change existing laws. Unlike in some other states, in Washington, the initiative process cannot be used to amend the constitution. There are two types of initiatives. An *initiative to the people*, once certified, is a proposed new law or change in existing law voted on in a general election. An *initiative to the legislature*, once certified, is a proposed new law or change in existing law submitted to the legislature. After certification, the legislature must (1) adopt the initiative as proposed, in which case it becomes law; (2) reject or refuse to act on the initiative, in which case it is put on the next general election ballot; or (3) approve an amended version of the proposed initiative, in which case both versions are put on the next general election ballot. To certify either type of initiative, the initiative's sponsor must collect enough signatures to equal eight percent of the number of votes cast for the office of Governor in the last regular gubernatorial election.

The referendum process gives voters the power to reject legislation proposed or adopted by the legislature. Just as there are two types of initiatives, there are two types of referenda. A *referendum bill* is a proposed law referred to the voters by the legislature. A *referendum measure* is a law recently passed by the legislature that is placed on the ballot because of petitions signed by voters. To certify a referendum measure, the referendum's sponsor must collect enough signatures to equal four percent of the number of votes cast for the office of Governor at the last regular gubernatorial election.

---

8. Wash. Const. art. II, § 1.

Useful resources for understanding these processes can be found on the "Initiatives & Referenda" section of the Secretary of State's "Elections and Voting" website (www.secstate.wa.gov/elections). There you will find a link to a document entitled "Filing Initiatives or Referenda in Washington State," which describes the overall process and provides step-by-step instructions. The website also includes the text of current initiatives and referenda and information (such as election results) on past initiatives and referenda.

When researching the history of a particular initiative or referendum, you can find some information on the legislature's "Bill Information" page (there are links for "Initiatives" and "Referenda" for recent bienniums). For older measures, use the print *Final Legislative Report* and the *Legislative Digest and History of Bills*.

The information that you will find depends on the kind of initiative that you are researching. Initiatives to the legislature will go through the usual legislative process and generate the usual legislative history documents. Initiatives to the people, if enacted, become law without going through the usual process, and so some of the usual documents are not created; nevertheless, you will find a report, similar to a final bill report, and a session law. Because initiatives are voted on in the general election in November, make sure you look at the information for the legislative session that begins the following January. Both types of referenda relate to bills that have already passed the legislature, so you will find the usual documents when researching referenda.

The voter's guide represents another important component of an initiative or referendum's legislative history. When examining laws created through the initiative or referendum process, you will want to read the voter's guide that was circulated during the election in which the measure was voted on. The voter's guide will contain a summary of the measure, an explanation of the current law and the effect of the measure, and statements for and against the measure. You can find archived guides from 1997 to present on the Secretary of State's website at (www.secstate.wa.gov/elections/voter_guides.aspx).

V. Federal Legislative Research[9]

The federal legislative process is comparable to the Washington legislative process. Many similar documents are produced, and you can use some of the same strategies you used in researching state legislation in researching federal legislation.

A. Federal Bill Tracking

Congressional material is increasingly available on the Internet, and using Internet sources for bill tracking is often easier than using print sources. The Thomas website, from the Library of Congress, (http://thomas.loc.gov) provides bill summaries and status, committee reports, and the *Congressional Record* (which records debate in the U.S. House and Senate). The Government Printing Office site (www.access.gpo.gov) contains bills, selected hearings and reports, and the *Congressional Record*. Coverage varies even within a single site, so check carefully.

B. Federal Legislative History

Researching federal legislative history involves roughly the same steps as researching Washington's laws, though some of the terminology is different. Bills are numbered sequentially in each chamber of Congress. Generally, Senate bill numbers are preceded by an "S," and House bill numbers are preceded by "H.R." When a federal statute is enacted, it is printed as a small booklet and assigned a *public law number*. This number is in the form "Pub. L. No. 101-336," where numbers before the hyphen are the number of the Congress in which the law was enacted, and the numbers after the hyphen are assigned chronologically as bills are enacted. The public law number given above is for the 1990 *Americans with Disabilities Act* (ADA), which was the 336th law passed during the 101st Congress.

---

9. Part V is based on materials drafted by Suzanne E. Rowe, editor, Carolina Academic Press Legal Research Series.

The new statute is later published as a session law in *United States Statutes at Large*, which is the federal counterpart to *Laws of Washington*. Session laws are designated by volume and page in *Statutes at Large*, e.g., 104 Stat. 328. Finally, the new statute gets another citation when it is codified with other statutes on similar topics in the United States Code. The code citation for the first section of the ADA is 42 USC § 12101.

As with Washington legislative history, you must begin federal legislative history with a statute number. With a code citation, you can find the session law citation and public law number, which will lead to the legislative history of the bill as it worked its way through Congress.

1. Sources of Federal Legislative History

In conducting federal legislative history research, you are looking for committee reports, materials from committee hearings, and transcripts of floor debates. Committee reports are considered the most persuasive authority. Congressional committee reports are often lengthy documents published in soft-cover format. These reports contain the committee's analysis of the bill, the reasons for enacting it, and the views of any members who disagree with those reasons. Congressional hearing materials include transcripts from the proceedings as well as documents such as prepared testimony and exhibits.

Floor debates are published in the *Congressional Record*. Be wary of relying on these debates when interpreting statutes, as they may not have actually been delivered in the House or Senate; members of Congress can amend their remarks and even submit written statements that are published in transcript form as if they were spoken.

Table 9.3 compares sources for Washington and federal legislative history.

2. Compiled Legislative History

Some researchers have *compiled* (assembled) legislative histories for certain federal statutes. Two reference books that compile legisla-

Table 9.3 Comparison of Sources for Washington and Federal Legislative History

Legislative Process	Washington Sources	Federal Sources
Committee work	Bill reports; recordings of committee hearings; information in the committee files	Committee reports; transcripts of hearings and other documents
Floor debate	*House Journal* and *Senate Journal*; both contain colloquies in addition to debate references	*Congressional Record* publishes the statements of the Senators and House members during debate
Session law (text of enacted statute)	*Laws of Washington*	*Statutes at Large*
Codified version	*Revised Code of Washington* (official) *Revised Code of Washington Annotated* *Annotated Revised Code of Washington*	*United States Code* (official) *United States Code Annotated* *United States Code Service*

tive histories of major federal statutes are *Sources of Compiled Legislative Histories*[10] and *Federal Legislative Histories*.[11]

3. Legislative Research in Print

Table 9.4 contains the most common print sources for researching federal legislative history. Some sources contain a "How to Use" section at the beginning; otherwise, ask a reference librarian.

10. Nancy P. Johnson, *Sources of Compiled Legislative Histories: A Bibliography of Government Documents, Periodical Articles, and Books* (2007). Your library might subscribe to this in HeinOnline.
11. Bernard D. Reams, Jr., *Federal Legislative Histories: An Annotated Bibliography and Index to Officially Published Sources* (1994).

Table 9.4 Selected Sources for Federal Legislative History in Print

Legislative History Source	Contents
United States Code Congressional and Administrative News Service (USCCAN)	Selected reprints and excerpts of committee reports; references to other reports and to the *Congressional Record*
Congressional Information Service (CIS)	Full text of bills, committee reports, and hearings on microfiche; print indexes and abstracts in bound volumes
Congressional Record	Debate from the floor of the House and Senate

4. Legislative Research Online

The websites noted earlier in this chapter for tracking federal legislation also provide useful information for legislative history research. The Thomas website (http://thomas.loc.gov) provides bill summaries and status, committee reports, and the *Congressional Record*. The Government Printing Office site (www.access.gpo.gov) contains bills, selected hearings and reports, as well as the *Congressional Record*.

Currently, fee-based sites such as Westlaw and LexisNexis have relatively few state legislative history documents, but they do have databases with federal materials such as committee reports, hearings, and the *Congressional Record*.

Chapter 10

Research Strategies and Organizing Research Results

I. Introduction[1]

In practice, a client will come into your office with a problem and ask you to help solve it. The client will tell you a story about what happened, focusing on facts that are important to him or her, without regard to whether they are legally significant. Your job will be to sift through this story to identify the legal issues. In doing so, you may need to ask questions to probe for facts the client may not immediately remember but which may have important legal consequences. You may also need to review documents such as contracts, letters, bills, or public records. In addition, you may need to interview other people who are involved in the client's situation.

Sometimes you will not be able to identify the legal issues immediately. Especially if you are dealing with an unfamiliar area of law, you may need to do some initial research to learn about the legal issues that affect the client's situation. Once you have some background in the relevant law, you should determine which legal issues affect the client's situation and begin to formulate a comprehensive research strategy.

---

1. Portions of this chapter were based on materials drafted by Suzanne E. Rowe, editor, Carolina Academic Press Legal Research Series.

II. Planning Your Research Strategy

The research process presented in Chapter 1 contains six steps: (1) generate a list of *research terms*; (2) do background reading in *secondary sources*; (3) find controlling *statutes, rules,* or *constitutional provisions* and use the *annotations* to find relevant cases; (4) use a *digest* or *online digest equivalent* to find citations to cases; if necessary, run a search in an online database; (5) *update* your legal authorities (using Shepard's or KeyCite); and (6) *assess* your research results. If the question is answered or the deadline is imminent, outline your legal analysis and begin writing your document. After learning how to use this process and how to use the different legal sources, you can customize your research process to meet the needs of your specific project.

When researching an unfamiliar area of law, you will probably be more successful if you start with secondary sources. In contrast, if you are familiar with an area of statutory law from previous work, your research may be more effective if you go directly to an annotated code. Or if you already know about a relevant case, you may want to begin by using case finding tools such as Shepard's or KeyCite or a West digest. These tools may quickly point you to more cases on point.

Whichever way you begin the research process, the process is unlikely to be linear. Sometimes you can skip steps. For example, secondary sources often cite relevant statutes, allowing you to bypass the code's index. At other times, the research process circles back on itself. For example, an annotated code may refer to a case that cites to a different statute. After you read those primary sources, you may want to return to secondary sources to review how the individual cases and statutes fit together. Even as you begin writing, you may need to do more research if new issues arise or you need more support for an argument.

III. Taking Notes

Take careful notes throughout the research process. You will probably find that taking useful notes is time consuming, but it will save you time in the end because you will avoid duplicating steps (especially if you have to interrupt your research for a period of time). Your notes also provide a basis for organizing and writing your analysis or argument. Do not underestimate the learning process that occurs while taking notes. The acts of deciding what is important enough to include in your notes and expressing those ideas in your own words will increase your understanding of the legal issues you are researching. Research consciously: merely clicking a "print" icon and highlighting (or underlining) text does not provide this analytical advantage. You need to actively process what you find.

The notes you produce as you research do not have to be formal or typed. In fact, you might waste time by creating too much structure or by stopping to type your notes. How to take organized and effective notes is discussed in more detail below.

IV. Organizing Your Research

Keeping your research organized increases efficiency, but it is not an end in itself. The only "right" way to organize your research is the way that best helps you perform effective research, understand the legal issues, and analyze the legal problem. Also, keep organization in perspective. Spending extra time may make you more efficient, or it may represent covert procrastination. Being in motion does not necessarily mean you are making progress; it may be a form of busy work.

The following method shows how to keep track of your research with either a binder or with folders and files on your computer. This section assumes that you will use a binder because this is usually an easier organization system for novice researchers. There are also tips on electronic organization if you decide to track your research on your computer.

Once you have your binder, make tabs for the binder with the following labels: (1) Research Plan, (2) Secondary Sources, (3) Statutes (include administrative rules and constitutional provisions here), (4) Cases, and (5) Updating. If you decide to organize your research on your computer, create a folder for your project and then create subfolders with the label names. The sections below explain what to put under each of these tabs (or in each subfolder).

When researching several issues or claims, consider them one at a time. If you are researching more than one issue or claim, you should have several sets of tabs in your binder (one set for each claim) or you should create different binders for each claim. Even when you are researching different elements within a single claim, you will probably want to consider them one at a time. Although you will probably not have a separate set of tabs for each element, you may have duplicates of at least some of your tabs.

For example, suppose you are researching an adverse possession claim in which there is a question about whether the possession was "hostile" and whether it was "continuous." In this circumstance, you will probably need only one tab for secondary sources and one tab for statutes. On the other hand, you will probably want two tabs for cases: one for the cases that discuss "hostile" and one for the cases that discuss "continuous." If a case addresses both elements, note it under both tabs.

A. Research Plan

No matter how many claims or elements you need to research, the first document you should create is your *research plan*. This plan may be a list of the legal resources you intend to examine or a template that helps you keep track of various elements of the project. Writing out your strategy also helps you break large, overwhelming projects into manageable steps. As you become a more experienced researcher, you probably will not need to write out the steps—they will become second nature. Before beginning your research, use the mnemonic device JUSTASK[2] as a checklist to save time, money, and effort:

- *Jurisdiction*: Is the issue governed by state law, federal law, or both?
- *Useful tips*: Did the assigning attorney mention experts in the field or statutes or constitutional provisions on point, or is this

---

2. See Ellen M. Callinan, *How to Survive Summer Associate Research ... and Thrive!—Advice from the Law Firm*, 7 Perspectives: Teaching Legal Res. & Writing 113 (1999), reprinted in *Best of Perspectives: Teaching Legal Research & Writing* 81 (2001).

a common law issue? Are administrative rules or decisions likely to be involved?

- *Scope of Research*: What period of time needs to be researched? How much information is needed? Should your research provide an overview or be exhaustive?
- *Terms of Art*: What are the standards terms in this area of law?
- *Acronyms*: Do you understand the meaning of acronyms used by the assigning attorney?
- *Sources*: What are the leading treatises, journals, or databases?
- *Key Cost Constraints*: How long do you have to complete the project? How many hours of online research can be billed?

Keep in mind that you may need to revise your plan as you learn more about the issues. For instance, you may read a case with a related cause of action that you had not considered, or you may encounter an article that highlights a relevant federal claim when you had been researching only a state claim. If so, adjust your research accordingly.

Your plan should include a list of research terms that you generate from the facts and issues of your research problem. Brainstorm and consider synonyms and antonyms to develop an expansive list. Refer to this list as you begin work in each new resource. Note on the list which terms were helpful in which resource. Add new terms to the list as you discover them, and note which terms do not seem to yield relevant results so you do not later think "why didn't I try searching _____?"

Next, begin your *research trail* or *research log*. While the research plan outlines what you intend to do, the research trail records what you actually search. Next to each step of your plan, write down the exact name of the source you use, the search terms that you look up, and the place in the source where you look for the search terms. For example, if you are researching in print, you may consult a practice guide as a secondary source. On your research plan, include the name of the practice guide, the search terms that you looked up, and whether you looked in the index, the table of contents, or both. If you are researching online, you may run a terms and connectors search in a case database. Either write down what you did or save and print your research trail. Both LexisNexis and Westlaw have tools to help you save a record of your searches. On Westlaw, click on the "Research Trail" link in the top right corner; on LexisNexis, click on the "History" link in the top right corner. Both services maintain a record of the search that you ran, and the database in which you ran it (e.g., Washington state cases) for at least two weeks.

Whether researching in print or online, keep track of both successful and unsuccessful searches. This prevents you from inadvertently repeating these steps later. It also allows you to revisit a "dead end" that later becomes relevant (you will be surprised at how often this happens). Finally, it prepares you to answer questions about your research path when you talk to colleagues or supervisors about your progress. Discussing your research intelligently is an important ingredient of professionalism.

Although tracking your research is time consuming, its importance cannot be overstated. Even when you no longer need to write down your research plan in advance, you should always document your research. This documentation helps prevent you from duplicating work. If you are unable to find anything on point, your supervisor's (or professor's) first two questions will probably be (1) "What sources did you look in?" and (2) "What research terms did you use?" Routinely reviewing your research documentation will help you think more strategically and help as a project-management tool.

B. Secondary Sources

Under this tab, keep your notes on the secondary sources you consult. For each secondary source, write a short summary. This summary should include information about the source itself and about the source's contents. Keep track of the name of the source and the page number on which you found the relevant information. Then, in your own words, summarize the relevant analysis in the source, including any references to primary authorities that may be on point.

One thing you will usually not want to do with a secondary source is make a copy or print out the full text. The goals of reading secondary sources are to obtain an overview of an area of law and to locate citations to primary authority. These goals can be met by referring to secondary sources in books or by skimming them online, without printing out numerous pages of text. Moreover, many law review articles that initially seem helpful may turn out to concentrate on a narrow point that is not applicable to your situation.

C. Primary Authorities

As you are reading secondary sources, looking up terms in a statutory index, or reviewing digest entries, create a list of primary authorities that you think are relevant. At regular intervals, stop and read the primary authority that you find. Legal analysis occurs throughout the process of researching a legal issue; reading as you research will ensure that you are finding relevant material and not just collecting clutter. Explore different modes of reading while you research: fast skimming to determine whether a source is even relevant; and slow, methodical reading to understand a relevant authority thoroughly.

Skim each authority first to decide whether it is relevant. Novice researchers may have trouble skimming efficiently because at first everything appears relevant. The following suggestions may help:

- If there is a constitutional provision, statute, or rule on point, begin by reading it carefully, and then move to reading cases that interpret the provision.
- For statutes and rules, skim through the sections that provide definitions or explain the purpose. Focus on language that sets out duties or prohibits certain conduct. Quickly glance at provisions codified just before or after your provisions to see whether they are relevant.
- For cases, first decide on an order in which to read them. One approach is to read cases in chronological order so that you see the development of the law over time. Because this may be time consuming for causes of action that have existed for many years, impose an artificial cut-off of twenty or thirty years in the past so that you can put your effort into recent

law. The opposite approach also works well in many situations. By beginning with recent cases, you avoid spending time learning old law that has been revised or superseded. In addition, newer cases often summarize the development of the law as it evolved from previous cases.

· When reading each case, begin by reading the synopsis at the beginning of the case. Then skim the headnotes to find the portion of the case that is on point. Go directly to that portion of the case and read it. This probably means skipping over the procedural history, the facts of the case, and analysis of unrelated points of law.

In the second, slower reading of relevant authorities, pay attention to parts that you may have skipped over earlier while skimming. Read definitions in statutes with particular care. Be sure you understand the procedural posture of each case because this affects how the court's analysis will apply to your situation. For example, if an appellate court announces a new test or rule, determine whether the appellate court applies that rule to the facts or remands the case back to the trial court to apply it. In the latter situation, you may not be able to make factual analogies between the reported case and your case. Drawing a timeline, chart of the relationships between the parties, or diagram (e.g., of disputed land) may also be helpful in understanding the case thoroughly.

1. Notes on Statutes and Rules

Your notes should include both the actual statutory or rule language and your outline of it. Because the exact wording of statutes and administrative rules is so important, you should print, photocopy, or electronically save the text of relevant statutes and rules. In addition, you should outline each of the main statutes and rules in order to make sure you fully understand them (some lawyers and professors call this "diagramming" a statute or rule). Highlighting is sufficient only if the statute or rule is very short and clear.

Finally, keep track of statutes and rules you read but do not think are relevant. For these provisions, you need to write down only the citation, a quick summary of the statute or rule, and, if not readily apparent from the summary, why you thought the provisions were not on point. This list, along with the statutes and rules you copied or printed and outlined, will become part of your research trail.

2. Notes on Cases

One of the best ways to keep track of relevant cases is with a case chart.[3] A case analysis chart allows the comparison of cases across categories of procedure, facts, rules, holding and reasoning. This comparison will help you see analogies and distinctions among cases. A case chart does not have to follow any particular format, but you will want to include the following information about each relevant case:

- *Citation.* Including the full citation will make writing your document easier and make finding the case again easier. It will also help your analysis because knowing which court decided a case and when the court decided the case helps you assess its strengths.

- *Procedural Posture.* The history of how this case arrived before this court.

- *Facts.* Unlike the case excerpts in class casebooks, full cases often include several issues. Include only the facts that are relevant to the issue you are researching.

- *Rules.* Include the legal rules that the court applies as it decides the issue you are researching.

- *Holding and Reasoning.* Summarize the court's analysis. Address only the issue that is relevant to your project. For example, if the case you are reading includes both a tort claim and a contract claim, but the contract claim is not relevant to your project, there is no need for you to thoroughly understand or take notes on the contract claim. Skim that section to be sure there is no relevant information hidden there, and then ignore it. Al-

---

3. *See* Tracy McGaugh, *The Synthesis Chart: Swiss Army Knife of Legal Writing*, 9 Perspectives: Teaching Legal Res. & Writing 80 (2001).

though focusing on part of a case may be unfamiliar to you, remember that you are reading the case to help you answer your client's question, not to be prepared for class.

In your chart, you will also want to include cases that you determine are not relevant. For these cases, you do not need to be as thorough as with the relevant cases, but you do want to include enough information so that you (1) do not waste time rereading the case to remember why you did not think it was on point and (2) can explain to a supervisor why you thought the case was not on point. As with your list and short summary of statutes and rules that you think are not pertinent, your chart entry and short summary of these cases will become part of your research trail.

You can organize your case chart in several different ways, but many researchers find it helpful to organize the cases chronologically. Chronological ordering helps you see the evolution of the rule over time. Because you will often find and read cases out of the order in which they were decided, use your computer to create your case chart; this way, you can insert new entries where necessary.

You do not need to print or save every case that you think is relevant. Sometimes a case is relevant only as background information, and your notes may contain enough information to use in writing your analysis. On the other hand, most researchers do copy, print, or save key cases. Doing so allows you to easily refer back to them and to double-check quotations. If you do print out a case, put it in your binder behind your case chart. Keep these cases in alphabetical order or in the order they appear in your case chart.

D. Updating

You will find yourself updating your research at several points during the research process. For example, you might use a citator as a finding tool early in the process to lead you to other relevant authorities (cases, statutes, regulations, and secondary sources). You will use a citator as a verification tool to ensure that each authority you include in your analysis is "good law." Even if you update your research during the research process, remember that you still need to update the law you rely on just before submitting a document. The law continually changes and may change while you are doing your research.

When you do your final update, it is often more efficient to update authorities in groups rather than one-by-one. Both LexisNexis and Westlaw have automated citation-checking tools: BriefCheck (LexisNexis) and WestCheck (Westlaw). These two services extract citations and quotations from your document (memorandum, brief, motion, or other pleading—or simply a list) and check their accuracy and validity. Both services provide a summary chart and detailed report. (See citator discussion in Chapter 7).

Whenever you check your citations, be sure to print out the results. Doing so makes it easy to compare new citations with the primary authorities that you have already read. On the printout record the date you searched the citator. If you print your results, keep them under your "Updating" tab, or put them behind each case under the "Cases" tab, in your research notebook. If you choose not to print your results, make a note on your case chart (or on the case itself) that you updated the case, and include the date you did the updating.

V. Outlining Your Analysis

Outlining your analysis before you start writing is critical. Because the most effective research often occurs in conjunction with analysis, begin to develop an outline that addresses your client's problem as early as you can in the research process. Your first outline may be based on information from a secondary source, the requirements of a statute, or the elements of a common law claim. As you continue researching, fill in the outline with statutes, cases, and analysis, but do not worry about using full citations, direct quotations, or even complete sentences. Instead, use the outline to arrange the different parts of the analysis and the different sources you uncovered in your research.

As you read the authorities and develop your outline, keep in mind that you are reading the authorities to help you solve a client's problem, not to be prepared for class. When you read a statute or case, ask yourself how it applies to the particular issue you are researching and the document you are writing. For example, as you read a statute, ask yourself whether the statute sets out elements or factors and whether these elements or factors can become subheadings and topics in your document. As you read a case, ask yourself whether the case (1) sets out the general rules that define the claim and its elements, (2) sets out the specific rules that define one of the elements, (3) involves a factual circumstance analogous to your client's circumstance, or (4) explains the policy reasons for allowing the claim.

Remember that research and analysis are not mutually exclusive skills or steps. As you do more research, you will refine your analysis; as you refine your analysis, you will uncover gaps in your research.

VI. Ending Your Research

The most difficult question many new researchers face is when to stop researching. Often, deadlines imposed by the court or a supervisor will limit the amount of time you can spend on a research project. The expense to the client will also be a consideration. Remember that no research is free, even when there's not a charge to retrieve material; the researcher's time is part of the cost-benefit analysis.

Apart from these practical considerations, most legal researchers want to believe that if they search long enough they will find the perfect case or statute or article that answers the client's legal question clearly and definitely. Sometimes that happens; if you find the answer, your research is over. If not, reaching one of the following points may help you decide that it is time to stop:

- New sources are not adding to your understanding of the law and are not factually analogous.
- New sources are citing back to the same statutes and cases.
- You come to the same answer to your legal question no matter which source you consult.

- The research cost exceeds its expected benefits.
- The project deadline is getting close.

If you reach one of these points, return to the original question and review your original research process. Have you covered each step of the basic research process (at the beginning of this chapter)? Have you begun circling back to the same unresolved questions? Do you thoroughly understand the issue and its dynamics?

If you have worked through the research process and found nothing, it may be that nothing exists. Before reaching that conclusion, expand your research terms and look in a few more secondary sources for leads to other authorities. You may want to consult with a colleague, a reference librarian, or your supervisor. This is where your research trail will help you avoid doing the same work twice. It will also show other legal professionals that you have researched your issue thoroughly.

As all the chapters in this book have shown, legal research is a challenging and dynamic endeavor. It requires thorough planning, persistence, and the willingness to think rigorously and creatively about the law. Learning to use the strategies and resources introduced in this book is just the beginning. Throughout your career you will need to keep up with new developments and refine your research skills. These efforts are worthwhile: effective legal research is critical for success in the legal profession.

Appendix A

Legal Citation[1]

To convince a reader that you thoroughly researched your argument and that your ideas are well supported, you must provide references to the authorities you used to develop your analysis and reach your conclusion. These references are called *legal citations*. Legal citations serve several purposes; among other things, these citations:

Table A.1 Purpose of Legal Citation

- show the reader where to find the cited material in the original case, statute, rule, article, or other authority.

- indicate the weight and persuasiveness of each authority, for example, by specifying the court that decided a case, the author of a document, or the publication date of the authority.

- convey the type and degree of support the authority offers, for example, by indicating whether the authority supports your point directly or only implicitly.

- demonstrate that the analysis in your document is the result of careful research.

- give credit to those who originated an idea you are presenting.

Source: Darby Dickerson & Ass'n of Legal Writing Dirs., *ALWD Citation Manual: A Professional System of Citation* (3d ed. 2006) (the "*ALWD Manual*").

Legal citations appear in the text of legal documents rather than in a bibliography. While you may initially feel that these citations clut-

---

1. This appendix is based on materials drafted by Suzanne E. Rowe, editor, Carolina Academic Press Legal Research Series.

ter your document, you will soon learn to appreciate the valuable information they provide.

The format used to convey that information, however, requires meticulous attention to detail. For example, you need to take notice of whether a space is needed between two abbreviations. In this respect, citation format rules can be like fundamental writing rules, which are based on convention, not reason. Why capitalize the personal pronoun "I," but not "we" or "you" or "they"? Why does a comma signify a pause, while a period indicates a stop? Rather than trying to understand why citations are formatted the way they are, the most practical approach is simply to learn citation rules and apply them. Frequent repetition will make them second nature.

Of the many different citation systems that exist, this appendix addresses one from a national citation manual called *The Bluebook*,[2] as well as the Washington citation rules (which are a modification of the rules found in *The Bluebook*). This appendix also briefly addresses a second national citation system found in the *ALWD Manual*, which is used to teach citation at some schools. The rules and explanations given below are not intended to be a comprehensive guide to citation. Instead, this appendix is intended to give you enough information to get started using proper citation and to become comfortable using some of the basic rules.

In law practice, you may encounter state statutes, court rules, and style manuals that dictate the form of citation used before the courts of different states. You may find that each firm or agency that you work for has its own preference for citation or makes minor variations to a generally accepted format. Some law offices have their own style manuals, drawn from state rules and national manuals. Once you learn what your employer's preferences are, adjust your citation format to that style. Learn the style of the teacher or journal you are writing for. Once you are aware of the basic function and format of citation, adapting to a slightly different set of rules will not be difficult.

---

2. *The Bluebook: A Uniform System of Citation* (Columbia Law Review Ass'n et al. eds., 18th ed. 2005) ("*The Bluebook*").

I. *The Bluebook*

Student editors of four Ivy League law reviews have developed the citation rules that are published as *The Bluebook*, now in its eighteenth edition. An author submitting an article for publication in one of those law reviews, or in any of the other law reviews that adhere to *The Bluebook*'s rules, should follow *Bluebook* citation format. In addition, Washington's citation rules follow *The Bluebook* with a limited list of exceptions.

A. Format of *The Bluebook*

The Bluebook has several sections, each with its own function. Table A.2 outlines the major sections, many of which are referred to throughout this appendix.

Table A.2 Sections of *The Bluebook*

Table of Contents and Index: Just like many other legal resources, *The Bluebook* has a table of contents (in the front) and an index (at the back). The index to *The Bluebook* is quite extensive, and in most instances it is more helpful than the table of contents. Usually, you should begin working with *The Bluebook* by referring to the index. Page numbers in black refer to citation instructions, while page numbers in blue refer to examples.

"Bluepages": The blue pages after the table of contents and a short introduction are called the "Bluepages." This section is a guide to basic citation for legal memos and court documents. In earlier editions of *The Bluebook*, this section was much shorter and was called "Practitioners' Notes." Many attorneys still call this section the "Practitioners' Notes."

Main Section: The white pages that follow the Bluepages are the main section of *The Bluebook*. This part of *The Bluebook* is more in depth and contains rules that are used (for the most part) in publishing law review articles. The Bluepages include references to these rules if you need more direction than the Bluepages provide.

Table A.2 Sections of *The Bluebook, continued*

Tables: Following the main section is a set of white pages with a blue border. These pages contain tables for use in conjunction with the rules in the Bluepages or the main section.* The rules tell you when to refer to the tables. The tables contain lists of abbreviations and explanations of which authority to cite. In citing cases and statutes, you will use the following tables most often:

- **Table 1 ("T.1")**—**United States Jurisdictions:** This table explains, for both federal and state materials, *which* authority to cite and *how* to cite this authority. For example, under the entry for "Washington," Table T.1 tells you to cite the official code when referencing a statute.

- **Table 6 ("T.6")**—**Case Names:** This table contains abbreviations for words in a party's name. For example, if the word "University" appears in a party's name, Table T.6 tells you to abbreviate it as "Univ."

- **Table 8 ("T.8")**—**Explanatory Phrases:** This table lists the phrases that tell the reader the subsequent history and weight of authority of a case. For example, if a case you are citing was later affirmed by a higher court, Table T.8 tells you to use the abbreviation "*aff'd*," to indicate this.

- **Table 10 ("T.10")**—**Geographical Terms:** This table provides the abbreviations for geographical locations. For example, Table T.10 tells you to abbreviate Washington as "Wash."

Quick Reference Guide: On the inside of the back cover is a "Quick Reference" guide that gives examples of citations used in legal memos and court documents. Examples of law review citations are inside the front cover.

---

* Do not confuse these tables with the two tables that are part of the Bluepages. The Bluepages tables contain a list of court document abbreviations and an index to jurisdiction-specific citation rules.

B. Citations for Memos and Court Documents (the "Bluepages")

As noted above, the rules most important to practicing attorneys—rules concerned with legal memos and court documents—are contained in the Bluepages. Because your first experience with doing your

Table A.3 Examples of Citation Sentences and Citation Clauses

---

Citation Sentences: Although owners of recreational land are immune from certain injury suits, a recreational landowner is not immune if the injuries were caused by a "known dangerous artificial latent condition" for which no warning signs were posted. Wash. Rev. Code § 4.24.210(4) (2004). The words "known," "dangerous," "artificial," and "latent" modify the word "condition" and not each other. *Van Dinter v. City of Kennewick*, 846 P.2d 522, 526 (Wash. 1993).

Citation Clauses: An owner of recreational land is liable for injuries caused by a "known dangerous artificial latent condition," Wash. Rev. Code § 4.24.210(4) (2004), and the words "known," "dangerous," "artificial," and "latent" modify the word "condition," not each other, *Van Dinter v. City of Kennewick*, 846 P.2d 522, 526 (Wash. 1993).

---

own citations will probably be in a legal memo, this section explains citations as described in the Bluepages. The next section then explains how citations in law review articles would be different.

1. Incorporating Citations into a Document

You must provide a citation for each idea that comes from a case, statute, article, or other source. A citation may offer support for an entire sentence or for only one idea expressed in the sentence. If the citation supports the entire sentence, it is placed in a separate *citation sentence* that begins with a capital letter and ends with a period. If the citation supports only a portion of the sentence, it is included immediately after the relevant part of that sentence and is set off from the sentence by commas in what is called a *citation clause*. Table A.3 provides examples of each, using *Bluebook* form.

When writing a memo, do not provide a citation for your client's facts or your conclusions about a case, statute, or other authority. For example, the following sentence should not be cited: "Under the facts presented, our client would not be liable because the bee hive was a natural condition." These facts and conclusions are unique to your situation and would not be found anywhere in the reference sources.

2. Case Citations

A full citation to a case includes: (1) the name of the case; (2) the volume and reporter in which the case is published; (3) the page number on which the case begins; (4) the exact page in the case that contains the idea that you are citing (this is called a *pinpoint citation* or *jump citation*); (5) the court that decided the case; (6) the year the case was decided; and (7) the subsequent history of a case, if any. The key conventions you need to know for citing cases are given below with examples.

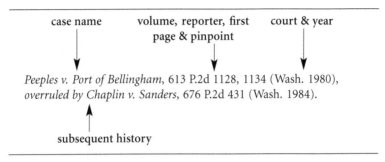

case name   volume, reporter, first   court & year
                          page & pinpoint

Peeples v. Port of Bellingham, 613 P.2d 1128, 1134 (Wash. 1980),
overruled by Chaplin v. Sanders, 676 P.2d 431 (Wash. 1984).

subsequent history

a. Essential Components of Case Citations

For the name of the case, use the name of only the first party listed on each side, even if several parties are listed in the case caption. If the party is an individual, include only the party's last name. If the party is not an individual, shorten the party's name (if possible) using the abbreviations in Table T.6. Note that to form a plural of an abbreviation, you simply add an "s." For example, the abbreviation for "Building" is "Bldg."; the abbreviation for "Buildings" is "Bldgs." Abbreviate geographical units (such as states) as indicated in Table T.10, unless the geographical unit is a named party. Thus, in Example 2, *New York* is not abbreviated as *N.Y.* because it is the party's name.

EXAMPLE 1: *Harris v. Fla. Elections Comm'n*, 235 F.3d 578, 580 (11th Cir. 2000).

EXAMPLE 2: *New York v. Belton*, 453 U.S. 454 (1981).
          Not *N.Y. v. Belton*

Between the parties' names, place a lower case "v" followed by a period. Do not use a capital "V" or the abbreviation "vs." Place a comma after the second party's name. Do not italicize or underline the comma.

In legal memos and court documents, the parties' names may be italicized or underlined. Use the style preferred by your supervisor, and use that style consistently throughout each document (e.g., do not combine italics and underlining within a single memo). (The authors of this book prefer italics.)

After the case name, give the volume and the reporter in which the case is found. Pay special attention to whether the reporter is in its first, second, or third series (e.g., *Pacific Reporter, Second Series* or *Pacific Reporter, Third Series*). Abbreviations for common reporters are found in Table T.1. This table is organized by jurisdiction, so to find a reporter abbreviation, go to the jurisdiction (e.g., Washington) where the case was decided. Note that in Table T.1, federal courts and their reporters are listed before state courts and their reporters.

After the reporter abbreviation, list the page number on which the case begins in the reporter, followed by a comma and a space, and then the pinpoint citation page. Remember that the pinpoint page is the page in the case that contains the idea you are referencing. If the pinpoint page you are citing is also the first page of the case, then the same page number will appear twice, even though this seems repetitive. If you are citing an entire case, you need not include a pinpoint citation.

In Example 1 above, "235" is the volume number, "F.3d" is the reporter abbreviation for *Federal Reporter, Third Series*, "578" is the first page of the decision, and "580" is the page the author wanted to reference.[3]

In parentheses following this information, indicate the court that decided the case and the year of the decision. Abbreviate the court

---

3. When using an online version of a case, keep in mind that a reference to a specific reporter page may change in the middle of a computer screen or printed page. Thus, the page number indicated at the top of the screen or page may not be the page where the relevant information is located. For example, if the notation *581 appeared in the text before the relevant information, the pinpoint citation would be to page 581, not page 580.

using the abbreviations in Table T.1 (court abbreviations are in parentheses after the name of each court). In Example 1 above, the Eleventh Circuit Court of Appeals, a federal court, decided the case.

There are two additional rules you should know for indicating which court decided a case. First, do not indicate the name of the court if it was the United States Supreme Court or the highest court of a state. If the United States Supreme Court decided the case, only the date should be in the parenthetical (see Example 2). If the highest court of a state decided the case, include only the name of the state and the date.

EXAMPLE 3: *Ketchum v. Moses*, 17 P.3d 735, 736 (Cal. 2001). **Not** (Cal. Sup. Ct. 2001)

Second, when citing state court decisions, omit the jurisdiction if it is unambiguously conveyed by the reporter title. For example, if you are citing a case in *Washington Reports*, you would not need to include "Wash." because the reporter title tells you the case was from a Washington court. Note that when read in combination with the rule in the previous paragraph, this rule means that if the highest court of the state rendered the decision, only the year will appear in the parenthetical.[4]

The final piece of information in most citations is the date the case was decided. For cases published in reporters, give only the year of the decision, not the month or date. In addition, make sure you are using the date of the court's decision, not the date on which the case was argued or submitted.

Sometimes a citation needs to show what happened to the case at a later stage of litigation. This is called the case's *subsequent history*.

---

4. You will probably see citations that contain only the date in the parentheses, but that do not seem to fall under this rule. It is common practice to omit the jurisdiction *and* name of the court if the reporter title unambiguously conveys this information (e.g., the reporter title *Washington Appellate Reports* would tell you that the case was decided by the Washington Court of Appeals). As you will see, the Washington citation rules (explained below) follow this practice.

For example, you may be citing a Washington Court of Appeals case that was reversed by the Washington Supreme Court, but on an issue different from the one for which you are using the case. As a general rule, always give the full subsequent history of a case. Remember that the subsequent history will be a part of your updating result in Shepard's or KeyCite (see Chapter 7).

To give the subsequent history of a case, put a comma after the court and date parenthetical, followed by the appropriate *explanatory phrase*. An explanatory phrase is an abbreviation indicating something procedural about the case. For example, one case may overrule another case. You can find a list of explanatory phrases in Table T.8; note that not all of them are followed by commas. An explanatory phrase should be in the same font as the case name (i.e., either italics or underlined), and it should be followed by a citation to another decision. If there are multiple decisions in the same year (for example, the case was decided by the Washington Court of Appeals and reversed by the Washington Supreme Court all in one year), include the year only once, in the final parentheses.

EXAMPLE 4: *Hoste v. Shanty Creek Mgmt., Inc.,* 561 N.W.2d 106, 109 (Mich. Ct. App. 1997), *rev'd,* 592 N.W.2d 360 (Mich. 1999).

There are a few exceptions to the rule that you should always include the full subsequent history. You should not include the denial of a discretionary appeal (e.g., a denial of certiorari) if the denial occurred more than two years ago. Remember from Chapter 1 that a losing party usually has a right to his or her first appeal, but must ask for any further appellate review. This further review is discretionary review. You should also omit any history on *remand* (when a case is sent back to a lower court for further proceedings) or a denial of a rehearing, unless particularly relevant to the point you are using the case to illustrate.

You only need to give the *prior history* of a case when it is significant to the point for which you are citing the case. For example, you may want to point out that your case reversed an earlier decision in that same litigation. Explanatory phrases for prior history are also included in Table T.8.

EXAMPLE 5:   The only time the Supreme Court addressed the requirement of motive for an EMTALA claim, the Court rejected that requirement. *Roberts v. Galen of Va., Inc.*, 525 U.S. 249, 253 (1999), *rev'g* 111 F.3d 405 (6th Cir. 1997).

b. Full and Short Citations to Cases

The first time you mention a case, you must immediately give its full citation, including all of the information outlined above. Even though it is technically correct to include the full citation at the beginning of a sentence, a full citation takes up considerable space. By the time your reader gets through the citation and to your idea at the end of the sentence, the reader may have lost interest. For that reason, try to write sentences that allow you to avoid putting the citation at the start of a sentence. The examples in Table A.4 illustrate this point.

After you have given the full citation, use a short citation to this same authority. A short citation omits some of the information in a full citation, but still allows the reader to find the page that you are referencing.

Table A.4 Examples of Full Citations

Assume that this is the first time the case has been mentioned in this document.

FAVORED: To bring a claim under the recreational use statute, a plaintiff must establish that an "artificial external circumstance so changed a natural condition it is unreasonable to distinguish the two when analyzing whether the condition was artificial." *Davis v. State*, 30 P.3d 460, 463 (Wash. 2001).

DISFAVORED: In *Davis v. State*, 30 P.3d 460, 463 (Wash. 2001), the Washington Supreme Court concluded that in order to bring a claim under the recreational use statute, a plaintiff must establish that an "artificial external circumstance so changed a natural condition it is unreasonable to distinguish the two when analyzing whether the condition was artificial."

The form of the short citation depends on (1) the page in the case that you are referencing and (2) the place in your document where the short citation appears.

If the immediately preceding citation is to the same case and the same page, use "*id.*" as the short citation. Capitalize this as "*Id.*" if it starts a citation sentence. If the immediately preceding citation is to a different page within the same case, follow the "*id.*" with "at" and then the new page number.

If the immediately preceding citation is not to the case you now want to reference, include in your short citation the name of one of the parties, the volume, the reporter abbreviation, and the word "at" followed by the pinpoint page. Generally, the first party named in the full citation is the party named in the short citation. Example 6 illustrates full and short citations, assuming the author has already cited to *Tennyson v. Plum Creek Timber Co.*, 872 P.2d 524 (Wash. Ct. App. 1994).

> EXAMPLE 6: As used in the recreational use statute, a "latent" condition "means [one] 'not readily apparent to the recreational user.'" *Ravenscroft v. Wash. Water Power Co.*, 969 P.2d 75, 82 (Wash. 1998) (quoting *Van Dinter v. City of Kennewick*, 846 P.2d 522, 526 (Wash. 1993)). "The condition itself, not the danger it poses, must be latent." *Id.* In addition, "[t]he dispositive question is whether the condition is readily apparent to the general class of recreational users, not whether one user might fail to discover it." *Id.* A particular user's reasonableness in failing to discover a condition has no bearing on whether the condition is latent. *Tennyson*, 872 P.2d at 527. This means that "a landowner is not required to anticipate the various ways that people might use its property." *Id.* at 528.

You cannot use *id.* if there is more than one source in the preceding citation. For purposes of this rule, citations within parentheticals (like the *Van Dinter* citation in Example 6) do not count as additional sources.

3. Statutes

a. State Statutes

Citations for state statutes generally provide three pieces of information: the code abbreviation, the number of the statute, and the date of the code. Each state has a different name for its official code. For example, although Washington calls its statutory compilation the "*Revised Code of Washington*," Oregon calls its statutory compilation "*Oregon Revised Statutes.*" In addition, most states have not only an official code, but also one or more unofficial versions of the code. For example, Washington's official code is the *Revised Code of Washington*, and its two unofficial codes are the *Revised Code of Washington Annotated* and the *Annotated Revised Code of Washington*.

For each state, Table T.1 of *The Bluebook* tells you which code to cite and how to cite this code. For Washington, the table says to cite "Wash. Rev. Code" (the official code). In addition, the table gives you the format for the citation: "Wash. Rev. Code § x (year)." In this format, there is a space between § and "x"; "x" is the statute's section number; and "year" is the year on the spine of the code volume (not the year the statute was enacted). Even if you do your research online, you will still need to check the print version of the code to determine the year to include in the citation.

EXAMPLE 7: Wash. Rev. Code § 4.24.210 (2004).

If your statute appears in the supplement to the main code volume, indicate this in the parenthetical by using the abbreviation "Supp." before the date. Note that because the Code Reviser publishes the entire code in even-numbered years, this situation should only arise in odd-numbered years or before the new version of the code is released in September.

EXAMPLE 8: Wash. Rev. Code § 18.06.130 (Supp. 2003).

The font used in Table T.1 is large and small capital letters. However, the Bluepages tell you that, for legal memos and court documents, you should use regular type.

b. Federal Statutes

Table T.1 also explains how to cite federal statutes. The generic rule is to cite the *United States Code* (USC), which is the official code for federal statutes. In reality, that publication is published so slowly that the current language will most likely be found in an unofficial commercial code, either *United States Code Annotated* (published by West) or *United States Code Service* (published by LexisNexis).

A citation to a federal statute includes the title number, code name, section number, publisher (except for USC), and year.[5] Like the date in a state statute citation, the date in a federal statute citation is the year of the code volume in which the statute was published, not the year the statute was enacted. In addition, just as with state statutes, you may have to cite a pocket part or other supplement. Example 9 provides illustrations of these rules.

> EXAMPLE 9: 28 U.S.C.A. §1332(b) (West Supp. 2008).
> [Statutory language appears in just the supplement.]
> 28 U.S.C.A. §1332 (West 1993 & Supp. 2008).
> [Statutory language appears in both the bound volume and the supplement.][6]

4. Signals

A citation must show the reader that you understand the level of support each authority provides. You do this by deciding whether to use an introductory *signal* and, if so, which one. The more commonly used signals are explained in Table A.5.

---

5. *The Bluebook* indicates that you should also include the name of the statute (e.g., the "Occupational Safety and Health Act (OSHA) of 1970") as part of a statutory citation when the statute is commonly cited that way or the information would help your reader identify the statute. In practice, however, attorneys tend to omit this extra information.

6. This citation results when the publisher includes only the changed portion of a statute in the supplement. For instance, in Example 9, the supplement includes subsection (b) in its entirety, but the supplement refers back to the main volume for other, unchanged portions of the statute.

Table A.5 Common Signals

No signal	The source directly states the proposition. The source identifies the source of a quotation. The source identifies an authority referred to in the text.
See	The source clearly supports the proposition. Use "*see*" instead of no signal when the proposition is not directly stated by the source but obviously follows from it. "*See*" indicates there is an inferential step between the authority cited and the proposition it supports.
See also	The source is additional material that supports the proposition.
E.g.,	Many authorities state the proposition, and you are citing only one or a few as examples. This signal lets you cite just one or a few sources while showing that many other sources state the same thing.

Source: *The Bluebook*, Rule 1.2

5. Parenthetical Information

At the end of a citation, you can append in parentheses additional information about the authority. This is called a *parenthetical*. Sometimes the parenthetical information conveys to the reader the weight of the authority. For example, a case may have been decided *en banc* or *per curiam*, or it may have been decided by a narrow split among the judges who heard the case. Similarly, use a parenthetical to indicate when you cite a case for a proposition that was not the holding of the majority (e.g., you are citing to a dissenting opinion).

EXAMPLE 10: *U.S. Term Limits, Inc. v. Thornton*, 514 U.S. 779, 884 (1995) (Thomas, J., dissenting).

A second use for parentheticals is to convey to the reader the relevance of a cited source when it may not be clear to the reader. When using this type of parenthetical, be sure that you do not inadvertently hide a critical part of the court's analysis at the end of a long citation, where a reader is likely to skip over it. Generally, this explanatory parenthetical should begin with a present participle (a verb that ends in "-ing") and start with a lower case letter.

EXAMPLE 11: A man-made change to a natural condition can create an "artificial" condition under the recreational use statute. *Ravenscroft v. Wash. Water Power Co.*, 969 P.2d 75, 82 (Wash. 1998) (finding defendant's acts of cutting down trees, leaving the stumps in a water channel, and raising the water level to cover stumps created an "artificial" condition).

You do not need to use a present participle if you are quoting material that reads as a full sentence. In this situation, the quotation should begin with a capital letter and include end punctuation.

EXAMPLE 12: However, not all man-made changes create "artificial" conditions under the statute. *Davis v. State*, 30 P.3d 460, 463 (Wash. 2001) ("[A] plaintiff must establish that the artificial external circumstance so changed a natural condition it is unreasonable to distinguish the two when analyzing whether the condition was artificial.").

In addition, sometimes a participle phrase is not necessary because of the context of the citation; in this situation, you can substitute a shorter parenthetical. For example, in a string of citations, you can sometimes include just a noun.

EXAMPLE 13: Courts have granted immunity to landowners even when the injury occurred on land that was not in its "natural" state. *See Chamberlain v. Dep't of Transp.*, 901 P.2d 344, 348 (Wash. Ct. App. 1995) (bridge); *Curran v. City of Marysville*, 766 P.2d 1141, 1144 (Wash. Ct. App. 1989) (park fitness and exercise court); *Riskem v. City of Seattle*, 736 P.2d 275, 277 (Wash. Ct. App. 1987) (bike and walking trail).

6. Quotations

Quotations should only be used when the reader needs to see the text exactly as it appears in the original authority. Excessive quotation has two drawbacks. First, quotations interrupt the flow of your writing when the style of the quoted language differs from your own. Second, excessive use of quotations may suggest to the reader that you do not fully comprehend the material; it is much easier to cut and paste together a document from pieces of various cases than it is to synthesize and explain a rule of law.

Of all the audiences you write for, trial courts will probably be most receptive to longer quotations. For example, quoting the controlling statutory language can be extremely helpful. As another example, if a well-known case explains an analytical point in a particularly insightful way, a quotation may be warranted.

When a quotation is needed, the words, punctuation, and capitalization within the quotation must appear exactly as they are in the original. Treat a quotation as a photocopy of the original text. Any alterations or omissions must be indicated, but always place commas and periods inside final quotation marks. Also, try to provide smooth transitions between your text and the quoted text. Make sure that the quoted materially fits grammatically within the sentence (e.g., make sure that the verb tense is correct).

If a quotation has fifty or more words, it must be indented on both sides and have justified margins, and it should not include quotation marks. Use the word count feature in your word processing program to quickly determine how many words are in a quotation. When you indent a quotation in this manner, put the citation at the very beginning of the line following the quotation, not indented along with the language of the quotation.

7. Noteworthy Details

Paying attention to the following details will enhance your reputation as a careful and conscientious lawyer.

Use proper ordinal abbreviations. The most confusing are 2d for "Second" and 3d for "Third" because they differ from the standard format. The tables in the back of *The Bluebook* indicate the proper ordinal abbreviations for reporters and other publications. Don't let your word processor make ordinal abbreviations superscript (use 1st, not 1st).

Do not insert a space between abbreviations of single capital letters. For example, there is no space in "U.S." Ordinal numbers like 2d and 3d are considered single capital letters for purposes of this rule. Thus, there is no space in P.2d or F.3d because 2d and 3d are considered single capital letters. Leave one space between elements of an abbreviation that are not single capital letters. For example, F. Supp. 2d has a space on each side of "Supp." It would be incorrect to write F.Supp.2d.

Remember that in citation sentences and clauses, you abbreviate case names using the abbreviations in Table T.6 and Table T.10. However, when using the case name in a textual sentence do not abbreviate these words. For example, although you would use *Harris v. Fla. Elections Comm'n* in a citation sentence (see Example 1), in a textual sentence this would be *Harris v. Florida Elections Commission*.

Generally, spell out numbers zero through ninety-nine, and use numerals for larger numbers. However, you should always spell out a number that is the first word of a sentence.

Watch your italicizing. The period after an "id." should be italicized. The comma that follows a case name in a case citation should not be italicized. These mistakes will be more obvious if you underline rather than use italics.

Do not use "*supra*" or "*infra*" to refer to a case that you have already cited or will cite later in the document. Although you may see this usage in some of the cases that you read, it is not correct under *Bluebook* rules. Instead, include the proper short citation form in either a citation clause or a citation sentence, as appropriate.

C. Citations for Law Review Articles

There are two major differences between law review citations and citations used for legal memos and court documents. First, law review articles place citations in footnotes or endnotes, instead of placing citations in the main text of a document. Second, most law review footnotes include text in three different typefaces: ordinary type, italics, and large and small capital letters.

The typeface used for a case name depends on (1) whether the case appears in the main text or in a footnote and (2) how the case is used. Case names may appear in either ordinary type or italics. When a case name appears in the main text of the article or in a textual sentence of a footnote, it is italicized. By contrast, if the case name appears in a footnote as part of a full citation in either a citation sentence or clause, the case name is written in ordinary type. If the case name in a footnote appears as part of a short citation, the case name is italicized.

Law review footnotes generally incorporate short citations in the same manner as other documents. The short citation "*id.*" can be used only if the preceding footnote contains just one authority. One unique *Bluebook* requirement is the "rule of five." This rule states that a short citation can be used only if the source is contained in the same footnote or is "*readily found in one of the preceding five footnotes*" in either full or short form (including "*id.*").

When citing a statute, usually the name of the code is in large and small capital letters. The abbreviations in Table T.1 for each state's code reflect the proper typeface.

II. Washington Citation Rules

As noted in the Bluepages, many courts have their own system of citation that may differ from *The Bluebook*. These rules are generically called "local rules." In Washington, these local rules are set out in a document called the *Style Sheet*.

A. The Washington *Style Sheet*

The *Style Sheet* is a two-page document published by the Office of Reporter of Decisions. This office prepares opinions for publishing in the official reports (*Washington Reports* and *Washington Appellate Reports*). The *Style Sheet* is the guide used in preparing the opinions.

The *Style Sheet* also applies to documents drafted by attorneys. General Rule 14 addresses the format for pleadings and other papers filed in all proceedings in all Washington Courts (trial and appellate).[7] Even if you are not working on a document that you will submit to a Washington court, your supervisor may want you to follow the rules on the *Style Sheet*.

You can obtain a copy of the *Style Sheet* on the Washington Courts website (www.courts.wa.gov). The *Style Sheet* is updated from time to time, so you should check periodically to see if you have the most recent version.

The *Style Sheet* instructs writers to follow *The Bluebook* except as it specifies. It includes general principles, a list of Washington-specific abbreviations, and exceptions and additions to *Bluebook* rules. If you have a question about how to cite a source using the *Style Sheet*, you can look at recent volumes of *Washington Reports, 2d Series* or *Washington Appellate Reports* to see how the Reporter of Decisions has cited the source. The sections below outline the most commonly used *Style Sheet* conventions.

B. Parallel Citations

When drafting anything other than documents submitted to a state court, *The Bluebook* instructs you to cite only the relevant regional reporter (such as *Pacific Reporter*). When drafting documents submitted to state courts, the Bluepages tell you to follow local rules for *parallel citations*. A parallel citation is a citation to a second or third

---

7. GR 14 was amended effective September 1, 2008. *See* www.courts.wa.gov/court_rules.

reporter where the case has been published. For example, a parallel citation for a Washington Supreme Court case would include information on where to find the case in *Washington Reports* and *Pacific Reporter*. Even though *The Bluebook* requires a citation to only the regional reporter, the *Style Sheet* requires parallel citations.

For Washington cases, the *Style Sheet* requires that you cite the official reporter along with the regional reporter. However, pinpoint citations for the *Pacific Reporter* are optional. You should not include the jurisdiction ("Wash.") or the name of the court (e.g., Ct. App.) in the date parenthetical.

> EXAMPLE 14: *Sheldon v. Fettig*, 129 Wn.2d 601, 607, 919 P.2d 1209 (1996).
>
> *Vukich v. Anderson*, 97 Wn. App. 684, 687, 985 P.2d 952 (1999).

For non-Washington cases, you need to cite both the official reporter and the regional reporter; pinpoint citations can be made to either the official or unofficial reporter, so long as you are consistent. For decisions of the United States Supreme Court, you must cite *United States Reports* (U.S.), *Supreme Court Reporter* (S. Ct.), and *Lawyer's Edition* (L. Ed. 2d), in that order.

> EXAMPLE 15: *U.S. Term Limits, Inc. v. Thornton*, 514 U.S. 779, 115 S. Ct. 1842, 131 L. Ed. 2d 881 (1995).

For short citations, you do not need a parallel citation; you only need to cite the official reporter.

> EXAMPLE 16: *Sheldon*, 129 Wn.2d at 607.

C. Other Differences Between *The Bluebook* and the *Style Sheet*

1. Abbreviations

The *Style Sheet* has a list of abbreviations for Washington materials that replaces the list of abbreviations in Table T.1 at the back of *The Bluebook*. The most frequently used abbreviations are listed in Table A.6.

Table A.6 Frequently Used Washington Abbreviations

Washington Constitution	Const. art. __, § __
Revised Code of Washington (official)	RCW
Revised Code of Washington Annotated (unofficial)	RCWA
Annotated Revised Code of Washington (unofficial)	ARCW
Washington Administrative Code	WAC
Washington Reports	Wash.
Washington Reports, 2d	Wn.2d
Washington Appellate Reports	Wn. App.

Notice that there are no periods in the abbreviations for any of the statutory compilations or the *Washington Administrative Code*. In addition, note that, although there are no spaces in "Wn.2d," there is a space in "Wn. App."

2. Statutes and Codes

Do not include the year in parentheses after a citation to a statute or code section if the statute or code section is currently in effect. Also, do not include a section symbol.

EXAMPLE 17: RCW 4.28.080.

   Not RCW § 4.24.080 (2004).

3. Numbers and Capitalization

Unlike under *The Bluebook* rules, under the *Style Sheet* rules, you should spell out only numbers one through nine. Use numerals (e.g., "10") for higher numbers. In addition, although specific *Bluebook* rules cover capitalization, the *Style Sheet* defers to *The Chicago Manual of Style*. Your library should have a copy of this popular writing manual.

III. Other States' Citation Rules

If you work in another state, follow that state's local rules or use the format given in *The Bluebook* or the *ALWD Manual* (discussed below), depending on your supervisor's preferences. For example, in Oregon, two sources of citation rules are the Uniform Trial Court Rules and the Oregon Appellate Courts' Style Manual. Similar to the abbreviations required by Washington's *Style Sheet*, the abbreviations required by the Oregon rules are familiar to lawyers practicing in that state, but may be confusing to lawyers elsewhere. To avoid confusion, ask your supervisor which citation form you should use.

IV. The *ALWD Manual*

The *ALWD Manual* is a newer national citation manual that was first published in 2000. It is now in its third edition, which was published in 2006. Many law schools have adopted the *ALWD Manual* because it uses a single system of citation for legal memos, court documents, and law review articles, thus making it easier for novices to use. No law schools in Washington have adopted the *ALWD Manual*, probably because the Washington citation rules are an adaptation of *The Bluebook*'s rules. Nevertheless, you should be aware of the *ALWD Manual* because of its rise in popularity.

There is often little or no difference between the final appearance of citations using the *ALWD Manual* and citations using *The Bluebook*'s rules for legal memos and court documents. Some of the most commonly encountered similarities and differences are explained below.

Appendices: The type of material contained in tables at the back of *The Bluebook* is contained in appendices at the back of the *ALWD Manual*.

Case Citations and Statutes: Case citations and statutes are virtually the same under *The Bluebook* and the *ALWD Manual*. The most obvious difference between the two concerns abbreviations used in case names. The list of abbreviations in *Bluebook* Table T.6 is much shorter than the list in the *ALWD Manual* abbreviation appendix. In addition, although some abbreviations in *The Bluebook* use apostrophes, all abbreviations in the *ALWD Manual* use periods. For example, the abbreviation for "Association" in *The Bluebook* is "Ass'n"; in the *ALWD Manual* it is "Assn."

Signals and Parenthetical Information: The rules for signals and parenthetical information are very similar.

Quotations: Similar to *The Bluebook*, the *ALWD Manual* requires indented blocks for quotations with fifty or more words. The *ALWD Manual* also allows indentation for quotations that span four or more lines of typed text.

You can find out more about the similarities and differences between *The Bluebook* and the *ALWD Manual* in several resources available at www.alwd.org/publications/citation_manual.htm.

V. Editing Citations

To be sure that the citations in your document correctly reflect your research and support your analysis, you should include enough time in the writing and editing process to check citation accuracy. As you are writing the document, refer to the local rules or to the citation manual required by your supervisor. In addition, after you have completely finished writing the text of the document, check the citations carefully again. When you do this check, you should not be checking for anything else (e.g., do not check your citations and your grammar at the same time). Be sure that each citation is still accurate after all the writing revisions you have made. For example, moving a sentence might require you to change an "*id.*" to another short citation form, or vice versa. In fact, some careful writers do not insert "*id.*" citations until they are completely finished writing and revising.

The time invested in citations is well spent if it enables the person reading your document to quickly find the authorities you cite and to understand your analysis. In addition, good citation form bolsters your reputation as a careful and conscientious attorney; one of the easiest ways to quickly lose credibility with a judge or supervisor is to have sloppy citations.

Appendix B

Selected Bibliography

J.D.S. Armstrong and Christopher A. Knott, *Where the Law Is: An Introduction to Advanced Legal Research* (3d ed. 2008).

Steven M. Barkan, Roy M. Mersky & Donald J. Dunn, *Fundamentals of Legal Research* (9th ed. 2009).

Robert C. Berring and Elizabeth A. Edinger, *Finding the Law* (12th ed. 2005).

Morris L. Cohen & Kent C. Olson, *Legal Research in a Nutshell* (9th ed. 2007).

Penny A. Hazelton et al., *Washington Legal Researcher's Deskbook 3d* (2002).

Penny A. Hazelton, ed., *Specialized Legal Research* (1987–2008).

Christina L. Kunz et al., *The Process of Legal Research* (7th ed. 2008).

LexisNexis, *Lessons in Legal Research: A Manual for Instructors* (3d ed. 2003).

Laurel Currie Oates, Anne Enquist & Kelly Kunsch, *The Legal Writing Handbook* (4th ed. 2006).

Laurel Currie Oates & Anne Enquist, *Just Research* (2005).

Suzanne E. Rowe, Series Editor, Legal Research Series (Carolina Academic Press). Titles include: *Oregon Legal Research* (2d ed. 2007); *California Legal Research* (2008); *Idaho Legal Research* (2008).

Appendix C

Commonly Used Washington Legal Research Abbreviations

ARCW (*Annotated Revised Code of Washington*) — a codification of Washington statutes published by LexisNexis. The ARCW, unlike the RCW, includes annotations. See Chapter 4.

MRSC (**Municipal Research & Services Center**) — a non-profit, independent organization that provides services to city and county governments in Washington. MRSC's website at www.legalWA.org has a searchable database of primary authority. See Chapter 2.

RAP (**Rules of Appellate Procedure**) — court rules that govern procedural issues in Washington's appellate courts. See Chapter 4.

RCW (*Revised Code of Washington*) — the official codification of Washington statutes published by the State of Washington. See Chapter 4.

RCWA (*Revised Code of Washington Annotated*) — a codification of Washington statutes published by West. The RCWA, unlike the RCW, includes annotations. See Chapter 4.

WAC (*Washington Administrative Code*) — the official codification of Washington's administrative regulations. Unlike the RCW, which has annotated counterparts, there is no annotated version of the WAC. See Chapter 8.

Wn.2d and Wash. 2d (*Washington Reports, Second Series*) — the abbreviations used for the reporter in which new decisions of the Washington Supreme Court are published. "Wn.2d" is the abbreviation required by Washington citation rules, while "Wash. 2d" is the abbreviation used in *The Bluebook* and the *ALWD*

Manual. Older decisions of the Washington Supreme Court (before 1939) are published in *Washington Reports*, which is abbreviated "Wash." under the Washington citation rules, *The Bluebook* rules, and the *ALWD* rules. See Chapter 5.

Wn. App. and Wash. App. (*Washington Appellate Reports*) — the abbreviations used for the reporter in which decisions of Washington's intermediate appellate court are published. "Wn. App." is the abbreviation required by Washington citation rules, while "Wash. App." is the abbreviation used in *The Bluebook* and the *ALWD Manual.* See Chapter 5.

About the Authors

Julie Heintz-Cho authored the first edition of *Washington Legal Research*. She taught in the Legal Writing Program at Seattle University School of Law, a program known for its innovative, practice-oriented legal writing curriculum and its process-oriented approach to teaching legal research. She is a graduate of Pepperdine School of Law and admitted to practice in Washington and Michigan.

Tom Cobb teaches legal research and writing, as well as evidence and immigration law, at the University of Washington School of Law. He began his legal career clerking for The Honorable Susan M. Leeson of the Oregon Supreme Court and then served as an Assistant Attorney General for the Oregon Department of Justice. He is a graduate of the University of Minnesota Law School.

Mary A. Hotchkiss teaches legal research at the University of Washington School of Law, where she is also an associate dean. A graduate of The George Washington University Law School, she worked at a Maryland law firm specializing in estate planning. She also served as a law librarian at the White House and the U.S. Court of Appeals, Ninth Circuit. She is the editor of *Perspectives: Teaching Legal Research & Writing*.

Index